Y0-BDW-180

ME
MY COUNTRY
MY GOD

DR. C. THOMAS ANDERSON
& DON ENEVOLDSEN

Winword
publishing house

Phoenix, Arizona

FIRST EDITION

Published by **Winword Publishing, Inc.**
3520 E. Brown Road, Mesa, AZ 85213
(480) 964-4GOD

ISBN 1-58588-048-5

Me, My Country, My God

Office number for book orders:

1-888-4WORDTV (1-888-496-7388)

or visit **www.winners.tv**

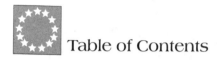 Table of Contents

 Introduction

Not like the brazen giant of Greek fame
With conquering limbs astride from land to land;
Here at our sea-washed, sunset gates shall stand
A mighty woman with a torch, whose flame
Is the imprisoned lightning, and her name
Mother of exiles. From her beacon-hand
Glows world-wide welcome; her mild eyes command
"Keep, ancient lands, your storied pomp!" cries she
With silent lips. "Give me your tired, your poor,
Your huddled masses yearning to breath free,
The wretched refuse of your teeming shore.
Send these, the homeless, tempest-tost, to me,
I lift my lamp beside the golden door!"
　　　　(The New Colossus" by Emma Lazarus)

　　America has never really been about Americans. It has always been about the "tired," the "poor," the "huddled masses" and the "wretched refuse" of the rest of the world who yearn to be free. For four centuries they have moved here to escape oppressive tyranny, to worship without compulsion and to flee the bondage of poverty. America is about those people – the refugees of every culture and nation on earth. America is not about Americans. It is about the world and it is about freedom.

　　The sonnet "The New Colossus" was inscribed at the base of the Statue of Liberty in 1903. Completed in 1884 and formally dedicated two years later by President Grover Cleveland, Lady Liberty towers 305 feet above the entrance to New York harbor. In her right hand, she holds a burning torch that represents liberty. The chains of tyranny lie at her feet. In her left hand is a tablet with the date "July 4, 1776" in Roman numerals. The seven rays of her crown represent the seven seas and continents.

The Statue of Liberty faces from Liberty Island across the harbor to Ellis Island where 12 million immigrants entered America between 1892 and 1954. The message is that the freedom which began on July 4, 1776 with the signing of the Declaration of Independence is not just for Americans. It is for everyone.

America is unique. There has never been a nation like it in all of history. From the earliest settlement at Jamestown in 1607, we can begin to identify characteristics that are America. It is the land of freedom. It is the land of opportunity. It is the land of equality. It is the land of free worship.

Jamestown was entirely intended to be a commercial venture licensed by the King of England. The second American settlement, further north at Plymouth, was also commercial but it was populated by people who sought the freedom to practice their worship without restraint.

These two characteristics are still what sets America apart. It is the richest nation in the world precisely because free enterprise and commercial venture are given such prominence. It is the one nation on earth where the freedom to worship without coercion by the government has always been valued. It is also the only nation that has consistently maintained a strong faith community without the law requiring it. America is a land of choice.

And it is a land of equality. Lincoln once described equality as the "central idea" of America.

Public opinion on any subject always has a "central idea" from which all its minor thoughts radiate . . . the "central idea" in our political public opinion at the beginning was and until recently has continued to be "the equality of men." (Abraham Lincoln)[1]

Alexis de Tocqueville, a Frenchman who traveled America in the 1830s, was struck by the degree to which Americans treated each other as equals, regardless of social position. The lowest on the social ladder refused to bow to the highest and the highest didn't seem to think that was anything out of order. It is difficult for most Americans to appreciate just how revolutionary this concept of life is without being familiar with the caste system of old Europe. In the Old World, you were free to succeed within your allotted place in life but you really never aspired to do anything else. In America, anyone can become successful in any area he chooses.

Add to these things the fact that the frontier life of early America was necessarily isolated from Europe. The government may have chartered the first settlements, but the people who made up those communities had an independent streak that they were not willing to relinquish without a fight. Even as early as the 1680s, attempts by the British to replace the original charter of Massachusetts with a royal governor were met with vehement opposition.[2] Separated as they were by thousands of miles of ocean, the colonists had to be self-sufficient. They could not count on help from anyone. That kind of an environment fosters independent thinking just as a matter of survival. From these factors we can get a pretty good idea why America has thrived. It has encouraged independent thinking and growth unlike any culture in history.

With abundance and freedom, however, comes responsibility. The United States of America is what it is because so many people for hundreds of years have accepted the challenge to mold it in the direction it has gone. If it is to continue, we who are living now must continue the vision that began so many years ago.

Our Constitution defines who is responsible for America.

> *We the people of the United States of America, in Order to form a more perfect Union, establish Justice, insure domestic Tranquility, provide for the common defense, promote the general Welfare, and secure the Blessings of Liberty to ourselves and our Posterity, do ordain and establish this Constitution for the United States of America.*

"We the people" are responsible. If this Union is to become more perfect, it is "we the people" who must make that happen. If justice is to be established, it is "we the people" who must establish it. If the nation is to experience domestic tranquility, it is "we the people" who must make it so. If the nation is to be defended and the general welfare promoted, it is "we the people" who must do it. If the blessings of liberty are to be secured for our families, it is "we the people" who must secure them.

One of the earliest experiments in social engineering was the Chautauqua Literary and Scientific Circle. In 1878, they announced a four-year guided reading program for ordinary citizens.[3] One of the most popular speeches associated with Chautauqua was titled "Responsibilities of the American Citizen." The speech announced that the greatest responsibility of a citizen was to listen to national leaders and get out of the way of progress.[4] That has been the focus of the American education system and the trend of society ever since the Civil War. It was not, however, the goal of the Founding Fathers when they created the Constitution. Neither is it consistent with the individual rights proclaimed in the Declaration of Independence or by the Constitution itself. Our Founders were never willing to sacrifice the individual.

Our purpose in this book is to examine the legacy that we have as Americans and to look at the responsibilities that we have as citizens to insure that we never lose our heritage. We will look at America through the eyes of our Founding Fathers in order to see the vision that compelled them to risk everything for the cause of freedom. We will examine in detail America's heritage in those areas that make us so unique – prosperity, freedom of conscience, equality and, most importantly, the biblical heritage that undergirds it all. We will look at the rights that each of us has as citizens but also at the responsibilities that are connected to those rights.

America has become a nation of liberal talkers but conservative givers. We have an anti-capitalistic movement of the masses but an expectation of big government financed by the capitalists. Those masses seek to limit the ability of the capitalists to make money but they still expect the capitalists to care for them and the poor through social medicine and equal housing. They want to punish the productive rich with increased taxes in order to soften the lives of the lazy and unproductive. They strive for a middle class caste system where all motivation and competition have been stifled so that everyone can have an equal share in the productivity of others. America has become dangerously socialist and the freedom to produce success is being gradually eroded.

Much of what we have to say is not politically correct. We prefer to stand for truth. Without truth, we are doomed to fail as a nation. Our desire is to see America become stronger than ever. But that means our responsibility as citizens becomes greater than ever.

---

[1]Quoted in Jaffa, *Original Intent and the Framers of the Constitution*, pg. 31.

[2]Lockridge, *A New England Town, The First Hundred Years*, pg. 87-88.

[3]Gatto, *The Underground History of American Education*, pg. 110.

[4]*Ibid*, pg. 112.

★★★★★

Individual Right #1:

The Right To Be Whatever You Want To Be

★★★★★

Responsibility #1:

Have Character and Virtue

★★★★★

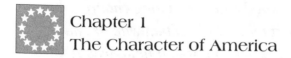

Chapter 1
The Character of America

Only a virtuous people are capable of freedom. As nations become corrupt and vicious, they have more need of masters. (Benjamin Franklin)

On November 19, 1863, President Abraham Lincoln stepped to the podium at the consecration of the new cemetery at Gettysburg, Pennsylvania. Four and a half months had passed since the bloody three-day battle there. It left 51,000 men wounded, dead or missing. Now most of those killed were buried around Lincoln and the crowd of onlookers who waited for him to address them.

The main attraction of the day was Edward Everett, one of the most popular speakers in America. He had delivered a two-hour address and finally sat down to wait for Lincoln to conclude the dedication.

Lincoln had only been invited three weeks before, almost as an afterthought, to make a "few appropriate remarks." He pulled a small piece of paper from his pocket and began to read.

Four score and seven years ago our fathers brought forth on this continent, a new nation, conceived in Liberty, and dedicated to the proposition that all men are created equal.

*Now we are engaged in a great civil war,
testing whether that nation, or any nation so
conceived and so dedicated, can long endure. We
are met on a great battle-field of that war. We have
come to dedicate a portion of that field, as a final
resting place for those who here gave their lives
that that nation might live. It is altogether fitting
and proper that we should do this.*

*But, in a larger sense, we can not dedicate –
we can not consecrate – we can not hallow – this
ground. The brave men, living and dead, who
struggled here, have consecrated it, far above our
poor power to add or detract. The world will little
note, nor long remember what we say here, but it
can never forget what they did here. It is for us
the living, rather, to be dedicated here to the
unfinished work which they who fought here have
thus far so nobly advanced. It is rather for us to
be here dedicated to the great task remaining
before us – that from these honored dead we take
increased devotion to that cause for which they
gave the last full measure of devotion – that we
here highly resolve that these dead shall not have
died in vain – that this nation, under God, shall
have a new birth of freedom – and that government
of the people, by the people, for the people, shall
not perish from the earth.*

It took only two minutes. The crowd, accustomed
to two-hour speeches, didn't realize he was finished. They
sat in stunned silence as Lincoln retreated to his chair.

He leaned over to a friend and said, "That speech won't scour. It is a flat failure."

Posterity has judged otherwise, however. It became one of the most memorable statements in history. The closing words, in particular, have been burned into the consciousness of every American, a reminder of one of the most basic tenets of the Declaration of Independence, that government existed by the "consent of the governed." Lincoln called it a "government of the people, by the people, for the people."

No government is simply imposed on us.

We get what we deserve.

Every American has heard these words. Most assume that they mean little more than a right to vote for government leaders. There is a much deeper truth implied, however. It portrays a great responsibility for every citizen.

A government of the people and by the people is one that reflects the values and the attitudes of the people. No government is simply imposed on us. We get what we deserve. If the president has no character, it is a reflection of the lack of character in the people. If the president has character, it is because the people have character. We must recognize that good government requires good people. And good people tend to have good government. Virtue is a responsibility.

Personal Accountability

We can find all kinds of opinions about how believers should relate to politics. Too many Christians feel that they should do nothing at all. Over the two national elections in 1996 and 2000, voting among evangelicals dropped 40 percent. Many others are not even registered. Only about one out of every four Christians votes.[1] Evangelicals turned out in record numbers for the 2004 elections but mainly because of the passion over homosexual marriage. It has generally required a debate over some moral issue to get them excited.

Such apathy has been a serious problem in America. Scripture identifies a direct connection between a government and its citizens that cannot be ignored. First of all, recognize that no government exists without God.

Let every soul be subject to the governing authorities. For there is no authority except from God, and the authorities that exist are appointed by God. Therefore whoever resists the authority resists the ordinance of God, and those who resist will bring judgment on themselves. (Romans 13:1, 2)

Peter reiterates the same thing, adding that we should submit to authority for the Lord's sake.

Therefore submit yourselves to every ordinance of man for the Lord's sake, whether to the king as supreme, or to governors, as to those who are sent by him for the punishment of evildoers and for the praise of those who do good. (1 Peter 2:13,-14)

Unfortunately, too many Christians read these verses without looking at the context and adopt a fatalistic attitude.

"It doesn't matter what I do. God will put whoever He wants into office anyway."

Let us establish a basic principle before continuing. God never does anything that absolves us of personal accountability. We are always responsible for decisions that we make. The death and the resurrection of Jesus made it possible for us to escape the consequences of sin but even then, we are responsible for making the decision to accept his sacrifice. God never imposes anything on us that we do not allow, not even government. God establishes governments, but he makes it clear how he chooses these. It is based on the people. Each of these commands to submit to the governmental authorities is in a context of righteousness.

Paul encouraged the Romans to righteous living. The verses preceding chapter 13 deal with the attitudes of godly people. He encourages them to love without hypocrisy, to abhor what is evil and to cling to what is good.

> *Do not be overcome by evil, but overcome evil with good.* (Romans 12:21)

The verses following the first part of chapter 13 talk about love.

> *Owe no one anything except to love one another.* (Romans 13:8)

Paul gave advice to Titus that had the same connection of virtue or moral character with submission to government.

Remind the people to be subject to rulers and authorities, to be obedient to be ready to do whatever is good, to slander no one, to be peaceable and considerate, and to show true humility toward all men. (Titus 3:1)

Peter places his comments about government in the same kind of context.

Beloved, I beg you as sojourners and pilgrims, abstain from fleshly lusts which war against the soul, having your conduct honorable among the Gentiles, that when they speak against you as evildoers, they may by your good works which they observe, glorify God in the day of visitation. (1 Peter 2:11-12)

The conduct of the people is inseparable from the government.

By the blessing of the upright the city is exalted, But it is overthrown by the mouth of the wicked.
(Proverbs 11:11)

God cautioned Israel to be careful how they lived, not just because sin would defile them. It would defile the land.

Do not defile yourselves with any of these things; for by all these the nations are defiled, which I am casting out before you. For the land is defiled. . . (Leviticus 18:24-25)

The graphic imagery of the Old Testament portrays what would happen when the land was defiled. The result of sin is expulsion.

> . . . lest the land vomit you out also when you defile it, as it vomited out the nations that were before you. (Leviticus 18:28)

The first responsibility of a citizen, then, may be the most important, even though it does not require that you run for office or involve yourself in politics in any way. Virtue and morality are absolutely essential.

It would not have taken much to save the cities of Sodom and Gomorrah. God would have held back the destruction if only ten righteous men had lived there.

> And He said, "I will not destroy it for the sake of ten." (Genesis 18:32)

And that is not ten men who were running for office on a platform to clean up the city. It required ten men who were righteous and who lived there. They would have an effect of the community around them just by their presence.

The Founding Fathers and Virtue

It is no wonder there are so many references to virtue and morality in the writings of the early leaders in America, those who put their lives on the line by signing the Declaration of Independence and those who framed the Constitution. A limited survey indicates just how much importance they placed on the quality of virtue.

It is religion and morality alone which can establish the principles upon which freedom can securely stand. The only foundation of a free constitution is pure virtue. (John Adams, signer of the Declaration of Independence and Second President of the United States)

We have no government armed with power capable of contending with human passions unbridled by morality and religion. . . . Our constitution was made only for a moral and religious people. It is wholly inadequate to the government of any other. (John Adams)

It is substantially true, that virtue or morality is a necessary spring of popular government. (George Washington, First President of the United States)

The federal government . . . can never be in danger of degenerating into a monarchy, an oligarchy, an aristocracy, or any other despotic or oppressive form so long as there shall remain any virtue in the body of the people. (George Washington)

To suppose that any form of government will secure liberty or happiness without virtue in the people is a chimerical idea. (James Madison, fourth President of the United States and "Father of the Constitution")

Neither the wisest constitution nor the wisest laws will secure the liberty and happiness of a people whose manners are universally corrupt. (Samuel Adams, signer of the Declaration of Independence)

Our liberty depends on our education, our laws, and habits . . . it is founded on morals and religion, whose authority reigns in the heart, and on the influence all these produce on public opinion before that opinion governs rulers. (Fisher Ames, Framer of the First Amendment)

It is certainly true that a popular government cannot flourish without virtue in the people. (Richard Henry Lee, Signer of the Declaration of Independence)

The only foundation for a useful education in a republic is to be laid in religion. Without this there can be no virtue, and without virtue there can be no liberty, and liberty is the object and life of all republican governments. (Benjamin Rush, Signer of the Declaration of Independence)

These are just a few of the multitude of quotes that could be given. Not all of these men were paragons of virtue, as we will see when we study some of them individually, but even the most ungodly of them understood that no government, not even one as carefully and brilliantly designed as America's, could work without the bulk of the population believing in a divine standard of right and wrong that governed the affairs of human beings. To fail in that belief would guarantee corruption. John Quincy Adams, the sixth president of the United States, expressed it this way:

> *There are three points of doctrine the belief of which forms the foundation of all morality. The first is the existence of God; the second is the immortality of the human soul; and the third is a future state of rewards and punishments. Suppose it possible for a man to disbelieve either of these three articles of faith and that man will have no conscience, he will have no other law than that of the tiger or the shark. The laws of man may bind him in chains or may put him to death, but they never can make him wise, virtuous, or happy.*

The Rights of Man

The French Revolution provides a notable example of a nation that abandoned a biblical and moral foundation. Starting in 1789, just a few years after the American Revolution, the French Revolution patterned itself after the Americans in a number of ways. "Liberty, Equality, Fraternity" became the rallying cry in the streets of Paris. A document was passed by the National Assembly on August 27, 1789 called the "Declaration of the Rights of Man." It was introduced by Lafayette, who had served with distinction in America under George Washington. Inspired by the American Bill of Rights and the Declaration of Independence, Lafayette, along with many others, wanted a similar statement to be a part of the new French Constitution.[2]

The American influence is obvious. Article 1 said, "Men are born and remain free and equal in rights." Article 2 echoed the words of the Declaration of Independence. "The aim of all political association is the preservation of the natural and imprescriptible rights of man. These rights are liberty, property, security, and resistance to oppression."

The great difference between France and America was the approach to worship. America's Founding Fathers declared that nothing would be allowed to infringe on the right to worship.

The French National Assembly determined to eliminate religion entirely. Church property was confiscated. Priests were imprisoned. The Cathedral of Notre-Dame was renamed the "Temple of Reason."[3] On November 23, 1793, all Christian churches in Paris were ordered to be closed.[4]

The most basic rights of man were trampled underfoot by the patriotic rhetoric.

The new Revolutionary calendar, imposed in September of 1792, created ten-day weeks, instead of seven, and abolished Sundays.[5]

The result of abandoning biblical virtue was that the French Revolution degenerated into the horrors of "The Terror" where the French beheaded 40,000 of their own citizens on the guillotine, often for such trivial offenses as wearing a royalist cockade.[6] Without the stabilizing influence of a biblical view of right and wrong, the Declaration of the Rights of Man quickly became a bloody sham. The most basic rights of man were trampled underfoot by the patriotic rhetoric.

Make no mistake. The same principle holds true for any nation. Every government reflects the values of the people. Perhaps de Tocqueville said it best.

I sought for the greatness and genius of America in her commodious harbors and her ample rivers, and it was not there; in her fertile fields and boundless prairies, and it was not there; in her rich mines and her vast world of commerce, and it was not there. Not until I went to the churches of America and heard her pulpits aflame with righteousness did I understand the secret of her genius and power. America is great because she is good, and if America ever ceases to be good, America will cease to be great.

---

[1] David Barton, "Wallbuilders.com".
[2] Durant, *The Age of Napoleon*, pg. 23.
[3] *Ibid.*, pg. 73.
[4] *Ibid.*
[5] *Voices of the French Revolution*, pg. 202-203.
[6] *Ibid.*, pg. 163.

★★★★★

Individual Right #2:

The Right To Pray

★★★★★

Responsibility #2:

Pray

★★★★★

 Chapter 2
If My People

In this situation of this Assembly, groping as it were in the dark to find political truth, and scarce able to distinguish it when presented to us, how has it happened, Sir, that we have not hitherto once thought of humbly applying to the Father of lights to illuminate our understandings? In the beginning of the Contest with G. Britain, when we were sensible of danger we had daily prayer in this room for the divine protection. – Our prayers, Sir, were heard, & they were graciously answered. (Benjamin Franklin to the Constitutional Convention, June 28, 1787)

In 1976, as part of the Bicentennial Celebration, artist Arnold Friberg, presented a painting titled "The Prayer at Valley Forge." It pictured George Washington, kneeling in prayer in the snow, his white horse standing patiently at his side. It was based on a story that first appeared in 1816 in a book by Reverend Mason L. Weems called *Life of George Washington, with Curious Anecdotes.*

According to the story, a local farmer named Isaac Potts was riding through the snow near Valley Forge. It was during the winter that the Continental Army camped there. Potts heard the sound of a man speaking in a wooded area nearby so he dismounted to investigate.

There in a clearing was George Washington, commander of the American army, kneeling in prayer for the victory of the Americans in the conflict with Britain.

Potts, a Tory at the time, hurried home to his wife and told her that the war was lost, that the British were beaten. When asked how he could be so sure, Potts exclaimed that the American army couldn't possibly be beaten when their commander-in-chief prayed as Washington did.

The story may or may not be true. The book it appeared in is a collection of far-fetched tales with very little historical support that have become a part of American folklore. They include stories such as Washington chopping down the cherry tree and the story of him throwing a coin over the Potomac River. The story was also told later by Reverend Nathaniel Randolph Snowden, a friend of Potts, who said Potts had told him the same thing. All things considered, it probably did not actually happen, at least not exactly that way.

★★★★★

Americans have a heritage
of turning to prayer
in the national interest.

★★★★★

There is another version of the same story that involved the Marquis de Lafayette and General Peter Muhlenberg. Both were part of the American army at Valley Forge and they became good friends, initially because they both spoke fluent French. The two men were riding along one day when they came to a barn that Washington used to stable his personal horses. Just a few days earlier, Washington had given Lafayette a horse that was still in the barn, so the two men decided to stop in and look at the horse.

According to the story, Lafayette laid his hand on the door and opened it, making no noise, but before he stepped inside, he saw Washington kneeling on some hay inside the barn, his hat on the ground at his side and his hands raised in prayer. Lafayette backed away quietly and the two men left without saying a word.

Neither of these two stories can be validated. If they are true, they have probably been embellished as legends always are and we probably cannot trust too much to the validity of the details.

But they also indicate that pretty much everyone had the idea that George Washington prayed. It was commonly thought that he often retired to some solitary location to seek God.

Americans have a heritage of turning to prayer in the national interest. It started from the very earliest colonies. Nearly the first thing the Pilgrims did when they walked ashore was to pray. Every time there was a crisis of any kind, the governors declared a day of fasting and prayer.

The Miracle of King George's War

Americans were used to seeing those prayers answered. The city of Boston experienced a dramatic divine intervention in a life or death crisis in 1746, thirty years before the American Revolution, a story with which all the Founding Fathers were familiar.[1]

It was during King George's war. The French in Louisburg prepared the largest fleet of ships ever assembled in the New World. The commander, Duc d'Anvill, had orders to take Cape Breton Island, then proceed to Boston and lay it in ashes, destroying as much as he could.

Boston had no hope of matching the military strength of the French, so the governor called for a day of fasting and prayer. People thronged to the churches. At the Old South Meeting house, Reverend Thomas Prince led hundreds of people in prayer. He asked God to deliver them from their enemies. He was very specific. "Send Thy tempest, Lord, upon the waters the eastward! Rise Thy right hand, Scatter the ships of our tormentors and drive them hence. Sink their proud frigates beneath the power of Thy winds!"

That morning was clear and calm, with plenty of sunshine. Reverend Price had barely uttered his prayer, however, when the sky darkened and the winds kicked up a violent storm that blew so hard it caused the bell in the steeple to ring twice.

Price looked up, raised his hands and thanked God for the answer. "We hear Thy voice, O Lord!" he cried out. "We hear it! Thy breath is upon the waters to the eastward, even upon the deep. Thy bell tolls for the dead of our enemies!"

A small ship sent out to watch the French came back with astonishing news. The French fleet had been virtually destroyed by the storm. D'Anvill was dead. The few ships that survived were half-manned with men who were sick from scurvy and fever. Thousands had been lost. They were limping away toward the West Indies, leaving Boston completely alone.

Franklin's Motion

Americans were accustomed to effective prayer. It was this heritage that Benjamin Franklin referred to in the speech quoted at the beginning of this chapter. He spoke at the Constitutional Convention. America, a brand new nation, found itself in a precarious position. The Continental Congress was unable to levy taxes and the individual states were not helping much. Nations such as Great Britain and France were having a very difficult time taking the United States seriously. There were British troops on the western frontier in forts that they were supposed to abandon at the end of the Revolutionary War. But they stayed and the Americans were too weak to force them out.

There was considerable unrest in some of the colonies. Martial law had been declared in Georgia. Savannah was threatened by the Creek Indians, stirred up by Spain. There was a rumor that a group in the New York legislature had secretly been communicating with the Viceroy of Canada. There were insurgents in Massachusetts. Rhode Island couldn't seem to get along with any of the other colonies at all.

Fifty-five delegates gathered in Philadelphia with the intention of trying to fix the Articles of Confederation, the system of government then in place, to give the Federal government enough strength to survive. Instead of fixing them, however, they ended up starting from scratch and creating a whole new constitution.

At the time that Franklin gave this particular speech, the convention had been deadlocked on several issues for more than a month. Some delegates had left in disgust. Others threatened to leave. There was an amazing lack of agreement about anything, perhaps not surprising, since thirty-four of the fifty-five delegates were lawyers.[2] It looked more and more like America might just fall apart.

That was the moment when Franklin stood to address the convention. His words are worth reading at length. He first addressed the problems facing them at that moment.

The small progress we have made after 4 or five weeks close attendance & continual reasonings with each other – our different sentiments on almost every question, several of the last producing as many noes as ays, is methinks a melancholy proof of the imperfection of the Human Understanding. We indeed seem to feel our own want of political wisdom, since we have been running about in search of it. We have gone back to ancient history for models of Government, and examined the different forms of those Republics which having been formed with the seeds of their own dissolution now no longer exist. And we have viewed Modern States all round Europe, but find none of their Constitutions suitable to our circumstances.[8]

He then asked the simple question, why they have not done the one thing that worked in the past, pointing out that in that very room, when the decision was made to go to war with Britain, it was prayer that guided them.

All of us who were engaged in the struggle must have observed frequent instances of a superintending providence in our favor. To that kind providence we owe this happy opportunity of consulting in peace on the means of establishing our future national felicity. And have we now forgotten that powerful friend? Or do we imagine that we no longer need his assistance? I have lived, Sir, a long time, and the longer I live, the more convincing proofs I see of this truth – that God Governs in the affairs of men. And if a sparrow cannot fall to the ground without his notice, is it probable that an empire can rise without his aid?[4]

Franklin then proposed that clergy be hired to begin each daily session by leading them in prayer.

We do not pretend to say that our Founding Fathers were perfect. They were not. People then were not much different than people now. They often had to be prodded to make godly decisions, as they do now. Even this incident, quoted so often, did not have quite the ending that Christians would have most liked. Roger Sherman seconded Franklin's motion but Alexander Hamilton and several others expressed an apprehension that "however proper such a resolution might have been at the beginning of the convention, it might at this late day, bring on it some disagreeable animadversions, & lead the public to believe that the embarrassments and dissensions within the Convention, had suggested this measure." They were worried that praying now, when they didn't at the beginning, would panic people into believing that things were really bad.

The delegates were reminded of the source of their success.

Ultimately the measure was dropped without even a vote. However, something changed that day, in spite of the official lack of vote. The delegates were reminded of the source of their success and many of them did pray on their own. It was a turning point, and the resolution of their differences started from that time. That was at the end of June, and the convention continued through September but it did not fall apart as so many had predicted.

These are just a few examples of the importance of prayer at critical times in American history. It is just as important now as it has ever been.

A Kingdom of Priests

The Bible makes it clear that prayer is something that has national implications.

> *When I shut up heaven and there is no rain, or command the locusts to devour the land, or send pestilence among My people, if My people who are called by My name will humble themselves, and pray and seek My face, and turn from their wicked ways, then I will hear from heaven, and will forgive their sin and heal their land.* (2 Chronicles 7:13, 14)

No matter what situation might face a nation, the answer is prayer. In biblical times, shutting up heaven so that there was no rain referred to an economic disaster. In an agricultural society, lack of rain could ruin the whole economic structure of the nation. Locusts stole the harvest before it could be enjoyed. Pestilence referred to disease that would cause the people to waste away.

America is no longer a strictly agricultural society, though the same types of plagues could affect American farmland. We have equivalent plagues that affect the cities. These include things like an economic recession, crime on our streets, violence in schools, epidemics like AIDES and the threat of terrorist attack.

We are not saying that everything bad that happens is a punishment of America for its sin. There are numerous factors that come into play. We do not believe that America is on the brink of destruction for its ungodliness. In fact, statistically, America is more "Christian" today than it has ever been. About 60 percent of Americans regularly attended church in the 1960s, up from 34 percent in the 1840s and up from as low as 15 percent in the 1600s.[5] We believe that America is stronger than ever.

But that does not mean that there are no problems. We recognize the attacks on the spiritual foundation of America and we know that many challenges exist. There is crime. There are economic failures. There is violence. There are terrorists. The solution is still prayer.

God said, "If My people . . .," meaning that it is the believers who matter in this, not anyone else. As with Sodom and Gomorrah, the preservation of the city depended on the righteous, not on the others. We cannot sit around and complain about the bad people who are causing so many problems. We have a responsibility as the people of God to do something ourselves. In particular, we are to humble ourselves, pray, seek God's face and turn from our wicked ways. It is not something incumbent on the other guy. America will not get better because the ungodly of the nation straighten themselves out. It will get better because God's people stop pointing fingers at sin and take on their responsibility to pray. (The truth is that there really is no other way to straighten out the ungodly anyway. We have to set the example.)

The next part of the process is to "humble" ourselves. The word in Hebrew is *kana'* (כָּנַע). It means to bend the knee or to humiliate. It has the idea of forced subjection. The implication in 2 Chronicles 7:14 is that we are to humiliate ourselves in the sense of forcing ourselves to bow before God in subjection to Him. That is the appropriate position before God for prayer, one that has no pride or arrogance, but rather an attitude of complete dependence on Him.

After humbling ourselves, we are to pray. The word here is *palal* (פָּלַל). It specifically refers to intercession for others. It has the root idea of judging, meaning that we are to assess the problem and then step in to intercede for it.

We are to seek God's face. The face, in Hebrew thinking, was literally "the part that turns." A face could look toward you or it could look away. It could look with favor or it could look with contempt. It is roughly the equivalent of saying that we are to seek the attention of God. Of course there is only one way to do that. Without faith, it is impossible to please God and faith comes from His Word. To seek his face, then, ultimately means knowing and living by the principles in the Word of God.

Note that this is not the kind of prayer in which we usually engage. It is not a request to God to take care of you and make you happy and comfortable. It is the prayer of intercession. It is interesting that God has always called His people priests. In the Old Testament, they were a kingdom of priests.

*And you shall be to Me a kingdom of priests
and a holy nation. These are the words which you
shall speak to the children of Israel. (Exodus 19:6)*

The same thing holds true for God's people today.

> *But you are a chosen generation, a royal priesthood, a holy nation, His own special people, that you may proclaim the praises of Him who called you out of darkness into His marvelous light.* (1 Peter 2:9)

A priest, called a *kohen* (ה) in the Old Testament, was defined as a person who stood in the place of another and pleaded his case.[6] As citizens of the kingdom of God, we have certain responsibilities toward the nation that we live in. It is not enough to sit back and complain about the state of the world. We must begin by having character and then we are responsible to pray over the nation as priests who plead the case of America before God. We need to bless the nation in the same way that God instructed Moses and Aaron to bless Israel.

> *Speak to Aaron and his sons, saying, "This is the way you shall bless the children of Israel. Say to them:*
>
> > *'The LORD bless you and keep you;*
> > *The LORD make His face shine upon you,*
> > *And be gracious to you;*
> > *The LORD lift up His countenance upon you,*
> > *And give you peace.'"*
>
> *So they shall put My name on the children of Israel, and I will bless them.* (Numbers 6:23-27)

[1]Bowen, *John Adams*, pg.

[2]Bowen, *Miracle at Philadelphia*, pg. 63.

[3]*Ibid.*, pg. 125.

[4]*Ibid.*, pg. 126.

[5]Shenkman, *I Love Paul Revere, Whether He Rode or Not*, pg. 22)

[6]Edersheim, *The Temple*, pg. 57.

★★★★★

Individual Right #3:

The Right To An Education

★★★★★

Responsibility #3:

Be Educated

★★★★★

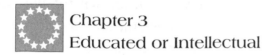

We are faced with the paradoxical fact that education has become one of the chief obstacles to intelligence and freedom of thought. (Bertrand Russell)

A story was told of a special banquet given by Cardinal Pedro González de Mendoza in which Christopher Columbus was the guest of honor. During the meal, one of the noblemen in attendance made the comment that Columbus had not really done anything unusual. It was just a matter of getting into a ship and sailing west until he ran into something. If he had not done it, someone else would have.

Columbus placed an egg on the table and asked if any present could make it stand on its end, unsupported. A few of the gentlemen tried, but after failing, they declared that it was impossible. At that point Columbus smashed the end of the egg to flatten it out. He then stood it upright on the broken end. Looking around the table, he said that it was really "the simplest thing in the world. Anyone can do it, after he has been shown how!"

Common sense is not all that common. In the most educated nation in history, it is frequently lacking. We have acquired immense amounts of information but we have no idea what to do with it. We can memorize things but we can't actually think. We find ourselves often in need of a Columbus to show us how and, to carry the analogy to its logical conclusion, the realm of reason is a new world to most.

In the past, Americans have been known for their problem-solving abilities. Irwin Rommel, the commander of the German forces in North Africa at the beginning of World War II, in assessing the qualities of the various armies that he faced, thought Americans the most dangerous precisely because of their tendency to innovation. His comment was that they knew less than anyone else about warfare when they started and learned faster than anyone else once they were in it. You just never knew what they were going to do.

We could cite dozens, even hundreds of examples of American innovation. Our history is filled with it. We have apocryphal stories about it. Perhaps you've heard the story of the truck and trailer that got stuck in a tunnel. It didn't quite have enough clearance. The best engineering experts and the greatest minds of the city were called in to figure out how to get it out. After hours of calculations and measurements to determine how much the tunnel would have to be widened in order to free the truck, a young child, with no formal education, suggested that they should just let the air out of the tires. The truck was free in a few minutes.

It demonstrates that there is a fundamental difference between learning information and understanding information, between being an intellectual and being educated. The Bible identifies it as a difference between knowledge and wisdom – and then declared that wisdom was the most important.

Wisdom is the principal thing:
Therefore get wisdom.
And in all your getting, get understanding.

*Exalt her, and she will promote you; She will bring
    you honor, when you embrace her.
She will place on your head an ornament of
    grace;
A crown of glory she will deliver to you.*
                    (Proverbs 4:7-9)

Most of Proverbs is devoted to comparing a wise man with a fool. A wise man has characteristics that enable him to grow and learn. A fool does not. A wise man has an open mind, a flexible reality, and the skill to turn new ideas into profit. A fool will believe every far-fetched scheme that comes along. A fool's reality does not have the ability to keep foolish ideas out.

A wise man knows his rights and knows how to defend those rights. He knows the ways of the human heart so well he is difficult to deceive or cheat. He understands the dynamics of human interaction and can form healthy, lasting relationships. A wise man can discover truth for himself.

In the context of modern America, we could call these two men by the names "educated" and "intellectual." It almost amounts to the same thing as wise and foolish. For this study, we are defining "intellectual" as a person with knowledge and "educated" as a person with the ability to reason and solve problems, to use knowledge for good. A wise man is one who learns how to think and to reason. A fool is one who simply learns facts but doesn't know what to do with them. A wise man is educated. A fool is intellectual. We realize that most people use the word education to refer simply to the process of going to school, but for our discussion, we are making the distinction that Douglas Yates recognized.

They say that we are better educated than our parents' generation. What they mean is that we go to school longer. They are not the same thing.
(Douglas Yates)

The Educated Mind

With this in mind, we can list some of the qualities of an educated person.

1. An educated person writes his own script for life.
2. An educated person is able to connect to the destiny that God has written on his heart. He is able to work his way through life to accomplish that destiny.
3. An educated person is self-determined and self-controlled.
4. An educated person has the ability to create new things, new experiences and new ideas.
5. An educated person creates a culture around the idea of freedom and responsibility.
6. An educated person can figure out how to be useful. He or she is disciplined and is willing to go to extreme lengths to fulfill his or her responsibility.
7. An educated person makes a list of things to stop doing and then focuses on what is most important and what he or she does best.
8. An educated person has an unwavering faith that he or she can and will prevail.
9. An educated person overcomes the curse of complacency and strives toward improving excellence.
10. An educated person needs little or no hierarchy to do his or her job with excellence.

These characteristics identify the educated person, the one who has learned to think and to reason rather than just learn facts. Mere intellectualism without education is not only a hindrance to growth and freedom, it is often dangerous. It leads to legalism and inflexibility. It keeps people from developing their talents and abilities so that they can grow in life. The intellectual has the appearance of education, but not the problem-solving skills. Note the differences in this comparison.

1. The educated seeks understanding. The intellectual seeks knowledge.
2. The educated can solve problems. The intellectual can only identify problems.
3. The educated is a dream completer. The intellectual is only a dreamer.
4. The educated is an overcomer. The intellectual is unchanging.
5. The educated is a conqueror. The intellectual is status quo.
6. The educated is an inventor. The intellectual is only a user.
7. The educated is a giver and a builder. The intellectual is a taker and a scrutinizer.
8. The educated is a thinker of possibilities. The intellectual is filled with impertinent facts.
9. The educated is a society improver. The intellectual is a society destroyer.
10. The educated is people-minded. The intellectual is things-oriented.

The unique qualities that made America great included the fact that early Americans were educated, not just intellectual. They learned the ability to learn. They did not just gain information. Our Founding Fathers were educated. Those who framed the Constitution of the United States were the most notable men in the country. They created an experiment in government that had never been done in all of history. They were innovative and they were brilliant. Thomas Jefferson, after looking at a list of the names of the delegates to the Constitutional Convention, called them "an assembly of demi-gods."[1]

It has become a place where we learn information but we are not taught how to think.

It is easy to attribute this brilliance to the quality of America's educational system. Unfortunately, however, most of those men had spent remarkably little time in school. George Washington barely had two years of formal schooling.

Benjamin Franklin, considered one of the most brilliant men in the world, even by those in France and Great Britain, was put into grammar school at the age of eight. He lasted about a year before he left. This man, who set up his own publishing house, published *The Pennsylvania Gazette*, produced *Poor Richard's Almanac*, delved into the scientific study of lightning, invented bifocals, reformed the postal system, represented America as an ambassador to France and Great Britain, and spent his childhood reading such books as *Pilgrim's Progress* and *Plutarch's Lives*, was a grade school drop out.

Abraham Lincoln, arguably the most articulate president in American history, had a mere fifty weeks of formal school, scattered over a twelve-year period from 1814 to 1826. Most of his learning was done on his own, lying in front of a fireplace at night with a book in his hands.

We could examine all of the great men of American history and we would almost universally find the same thing. Their brilliance and their education did not come from a school classroom. In fact, for most of them, there was no formal classroom available. They had to learn on the job. The system of education that we have in place today has actually resulted in education taking longer and accomplishing less. It has become a place where we learn information but we are not taught how to think.

We need to look at the history of American education in order to identify areas in which we have become deficient. For most of us, it will mean that we need to learn to think in ways that school never taught us. We need to develop the ability to analyze, reason and solve problems. Without this ability, it will prove impossible for us to even judge the qualities of a presidential candidate, much less contribute to the good of our community. We have to become educated.

Information Replacing Wisdom

Most people have heard some variation of the saying "He who can, does. He who cannot, teaches." Most do not realize that these words came from a pretty well known British writer, George Bernard Shaw. Another British dramatist and poet expressed almost the same sentiment.

Everyone who is incapable of learning has taken to teaching. (Oscar Wilde)

We are not saying that all teachers are incompetent. There are many excellent teachers out there. It is the whole concept of teaching that is the problem. Many teachers have understood the difference between feeding facts to a room of students and actually challenging them to learn and to think. But these teachers are usually running contrary to the system as it exists in America today. The goals of classroom education are not usually to make kids think. They are rather to establish conformity to the standards and lifestyle of the culture.

It is interesting to peruse the comments of a variety of philosophers, writers, artists and businessmen about the educational system in the Western world. It is difficult to find any who really think much of it. Some are humorous.

Lectures make one numb at both ends. (Mark Twain)

Another of Twain's comments is often repeated.

I have never let my schooling interfere with my education. (Mark Twain)

Many are more serious.

We are shut up in schools and college recitation rooms for ten or fifteen years, and come out at last with a bellyful of words and do not know a thing. (Ralph Waldo Emerson)

The great minds of history recognized that, just like Washington and Franklin, the important things in life were learned through the effort of the individual. Just knowing information is not enough. There must also be the wisdom of practical application or it is useless knowledge.

> *Nothing in education is so astonishing as the amount of ignorance it accumulates in the form of inert facts.* (Henry Brooks Adams, historian and writer)

Ben Franklin had a knack for getting to the root of the problem without quite coming out and saying it. He described a man for whom he apparently had very little respect.

> *He was so learned that he could name a horse in nine languages; so ignorant that he bought a cow to ride on.* (Benjamin Franklin)

And this is nothing new. In the 1600s, George Savile, the first Marquis of Halifax, recognized the uselessness of mere facts without understanding.

> *The vanity of teaching often tempteth a man to forget he is a blockhead.* (George Savile)

Writing in the first century, Petronius hit on the biggest part of the problem.

> *I'm sure the reason such young nitwits are produced in our schools is because they have no*

contact with anything of any use in everyday life.
(Petronius in *The Satyricon*)

The point we are making in all of this is that education is not a matter of learning information. It requires learning wisdom. Most of what you need to know to be successful in life and to be a responsible citizen will not come from the classroom. It will come from developing your own drive to learn and from spending your own time reading and growing.

It takes a certain amount of self-discipline. Dr. Myles Munroe defined college as a place where you pay them to make you read the books that you did not have enough self-discipline to read on your own. John Adams once said, "I have never been afraid of a book."[2] It is not just a matter of going to school, however. It requires an effort on your part toward discernment. No one can make you learn to think, no matter how many facts they cram into your head.

Real education must ultimately be limited to men who insist on knowing – the rest is mere sheep-herding. (Ezra Loomis Pound, American poet)

A look at the history of our school system will give a better idea of how we got to this point. For a comprehensive study we refer you to the work of John Taylor Gatto, especially *The Underground History of Education.* We can give only a brief synopsis here.

The purpose of education in a free society originally was to produce children who were self-sufficient, creative, self-motivated and who had understanding and wisdom. The goal of a good teacher is to entice students into constantly asking questions and seeking answers.

Unfortunately, the goal of public education is often just the opposite. Common schooling, meaning a public school where all the children of the community are required to go, historically has been designed to create students who are regimented and submitted to some kind of a cultural norm. Such a system does not want individual thought. It wants everyone to be the same. It strives for conformity.

The American system of schooling can be traced historically to India and the Hindu caste system. It was a man named Andrew Bell, an Anglican chaplain working in India during the late eigh-

The purpose of education in a free society originally was to produce children who were self-sufficient.

teenth century as part of the British colonial empire, who first described the Hindu educational patterns to the Western world. He was particularly interested in studying the Hindu caste system.

This structure of Indian society had five basic castes. At the top were the Brahmins, a class of priests who took care of things like law, medicine and teaching. Below them was the warrior class, who carried the administrative responsibilities, and the industrial caste. These three classes only encompassed about 5 percent of the total population. The other 95 percent belonged to the menial caste and the "untouchables."

The purpose of schooling in India was to preserve the caste system. The upper tier was taught to think, to analyze and to reason. They had to in order to exercise their authority and run the nation. What developed for the other classes was a kind of mass schooling in which hundreds of children were brought together into a room and divided into groups of ten under the direction of student leaders. A Brahmin directed the whole assembly.

The children were required to memorize the facts that would create attitudes of subservience and a willingness to stay within their proper place in the society and never think about moving up to another class. It was learning designed to produce workers, not leaders. Bell observed that they actually seemed relieved to not have to think. Life became a simple adherence to everyday ritual and routine and required no responsibility from them other than to do what they were told.

Bell published a pamphlet in 1797, describing his experiences and observations. He proclaimed the benefits of Hindu ritual as an impediment to learning writing and ciphering and an effective way to control reading development. Bell had the idea that this system would be perfect for the growing industrial society in Britain, where there was not a need for self-reliant, thinking citizens, but rather for docile factory workers who would be happy with their lot in life.

It all came to America through a Quaker named Joseph Lancaster, who read Bell's account and somehow got the idea that this Hindu system would actually help to awaken intellect in the lower classes of London. He gathered poor children into a free school where he gave them a rudimentary instruction. Word spread and soon there were a thousand children seeking this education.

What attracted the most attention to the Lancaster schools, however, was not the educational opportunities, but the remarkably cheap budget required to run them. One teacher could take care of a large number of children. It was recognized by numerous leaders as a way to control a population and keep the factories full. All you had to do was teach facts that made them good workers and never teach anyone how to think. As the children grew, they would assume that this life was their destiny and they would be content to stay right there. They would remain poor because they believed it was God's will and that it was their lot in life.

After some financial setbacks, Lancaster moved to America and instituted the same system here. It had the same effect. Children grew up learning more facts but with less understanding and less problem-solving skills, more knowledge and less wisdom.

Industrial America

In the years leading up to the Civil War, southern criticism of the North centered on the idea that northern industry was designed to create a class of white slaves who did their menial tasks in the factories. In 1858, Senator James H. Hammond of South Carolina gave a famous speech in which he labeled the northern workers "mud-sills." He believed southern culture was superior to northern culture because, by assigning black slaves to the role of workers, they avoided the conflicts between white workers and white capitalists.[3]

Your whole hireling class of manual laborers and "operatives," as you call them, are essentially slaves.[4]

The comments of Senator Hammond and other Confederate leaders illustrate the degree to which industry changed the United States. The Civil War became the point of transition. Before the war, America was an agricultural society with growing industry. After the war, the progress of industry took precedence over everything else.

William T. Sherman was such a popular war hero that both political parties tried to draft him as their presidential candidate. The Republicans spoke of nominating him in 1876, 1880 and 1884. The Democrats considered him in 1868 and 1872. He declined all offers, sometimes in humorous ways. In 1884, he sent a telegram to a friend at the Republican convention that read, "I will not accept if nominated, and will not serve if elected."[5] Sherman epitomized the new America. He had a settled belief in the destiny of America in which conformity and order were more important than the individual.

After the war, the progress of industry took precedence over everything else.

Sherman served as an officer on the staff of the military governor of California during the California Gold Rush in the 1840s. He witnessed a situation that bordered on anarchy, "the chaos of 1849-50," to use Sherman's own words. The military became the only real governmental authority and the only check to the gold-seekers pillaging one another. Most objectionable to Sherman was the formation of an extra-legal government by a group called the San Francisco Committee of Vigilance in 1856. It opposed the governor and punished its political enemies and, for the most part, got away with it.[6]

This experience was only confirmed for Sherman by the Civil War. In his mind, law and order became the primary features of the American way of life. The Civil War was, in Sherman's view and in the view of most northerners, a struggle to maintain law and order.

> *I am and always have been an active defender of law & the constitution. Twice have I sacrificed myself thereto. In San Francisco to a Northern mob, and in Louisiana to a Southern rebellion.*[7]

American Industrialists

The goal of social order became a national trend after the war and it was reflected in the development of the education system. It can be seen especially in the twentieth century as industry became increasingly dominant. The stated purpose of many of the industrial leaders of the early twentieth century was not the maintenance of the freedoms of America or even the amassing of great fortunes but rather the development of a class of workers. Equality became secondary. Before World War I, Woodrow Wilson delineated this in a speech to businessmen.

> *We want one class to have a liberal education. We want another class, a very much larger class of necessity, to forgo the privilege of a liberal education and fit themselves to perform specific difficult manual tasks.*[8]

By 1917, a group was formed to promote what British evolutionist Benjamin Kidd called the intention to "impose on the young the ideal of subordination."[9] It was called "the Education Trust." Its first meeting included representatives of some of the most prominent and recognizable names in American business and education – Rockefeller, Carnegie, Harvard, Stanford, the University of Chicago and the National Education Association.[10]

It is sobering to see the purpose that was intended by some of these renowned figures of public trust. Names that have been lauded in our history as progressive, far-sighted entrepreneurs frequently had an agenda that was counter to the principles of personal freedom that our Founding Fathers intended.

Henry Ford is best known for his development of the assembly line. It revolutionized industry. His goals went far beyond just making cars, however. He conceived a regimented life style in which everyone became a cog in the machine. He espoused this philosophy in two essays written in the 1920s, *The Meaning of Time* and *Machinery: the New Messiah*.[11]

> *A clean factory, clean tools, accurate gauges, and precise methods of manufacture produce a smooth working efficient machine [just as] clean thinking, clean living, and square dealing make for a decent home life.* (Henry Ford)

Like other industrialists and educators in the Education Trust, Ford saw his role in society not as protecting freedom but rather as social engineering that would dumb down the population to make them better factory workers. This was not a simple desire for power. It was rather the belief that society would benefit as a whole from limiting education. His underlying beliefs can be seen in a comment he made in 1929. "A great business is really too big to be human."[12]

Ford lived at a time when immigrants were pouring into America from a variety of countries, especially from Europe. Ford welcomed them into his factories, but his emphasis was on making them all think the same so that they fit into American industry. The last thing he wanted was a bunch of individuals. Ford's views on regimented society, where the individual lost any sense of personal identity and became a mindless servant of the nation, were inspiration for several tyrants of history. Adolf Hitler, for example, praised him frequently.[13]

John D. Rockefeller is another name familiar to every American. For much the same reasons as Ford, he supported the proliferation of forced schooling. He and other wealthy industrialists spent more on the development of forced schooling than the government did. He wanted to mold society. This paragraph is from a mission statement by Rockefeller's General Education Board called *Occasional Letter Number One*. It was written in 1906.

> *In our dreams . . . people yield themselves with perfect docility to our molding hands. The present educational conventions [intellectual and character education] fade from our minds, and unhampered by tradition we work our own good will upon a grateful and responsive folk. We shall not try to make these people or any of their children into philosophers or men of learning or men of science. We have not to raise up from*

among them authors, educators, poets or men of letters. We shall not search for embryo great artists, painters, musicians, nor lawyers, doctors, preachers, politicians, statesmen, of whom we have ample supply. The task we set before ourselves is very simple . . . we will organize children . . . and teach them to do in a perfect way the things their fathers and mothers are doing in an imperfect way.[14]

Andrew Carnegie, who made his fortune in the steel industry, proclaimed the idea of a "Gospel of Wealth." The concept found immediate acceptance by his peers. He believed that the wealthy owed a duty to society to take over everything in the public interest.[15] Like Ford and Rockefeller, he had an almost religious belief in the destiny of American Industry to form a world order that would replace the Christian world-view that preceded it.

The Prussian System

The social elite of America had for some time stood in admiration of the Prussian system of education. Prussia was noted in history for its militaristic society. Under Frederick the Great, the Prussian army proved to be consistently formidable against overwhelming odds. Writers of the time commented on the precision and order with which the Prussians moved on the battlefield. Everything about the Prussian system illustrated order. In fact, prior to the 1730s, no army in Europe made use of cadenced marching. It was first introduced into the Prussian army by Leopold of Anhalt-Dessau and was one of the primary ingredients in the machine-like efficiency of the Prussian military.[16]

The reputation of the Prussian army was destroyed in 1807 when it completely disintegrated in the face of Napoleon's French forces. The humiliation was so complete that, in the wake of the Napoleonic period, a system of school was instituted that required every child to attend, something that had not been done before anywhere. The Prussian Reform Movement set out to regiment the children of the nation and produce "good" cit-

Under the guise of education for all, the masses were taught to be obedient rather than to think.

izens who could support the nation. Efficiency was emphasized over education. Under the guise of education for all, the masses were taught to be obedient rather than to think.

The American Education Trust modeled their goals on the Prussian method. It seemed like a good thing for everyone, since it guaranteed that every American child would receive an education. Under the U.S. Commissioner of Education between 1889 and 1906, the school system was standardized and more and more American children were required to attend for a longer period of time, all to create a mindset that was more committed to the state at the expense of the individual.

The result has been devastating to the ability of the average American to think for himself. John Taylor Gatto cites the results of literacy evaluations for men joining the army, a test designed to make sure that soldiers have a minimum ability to accomplish such basic things as understanding orders and interpreting road signs.

In 1930, it was found that 98 percent of the applicants had a reading level adequate for military service. Ten years later, at the beginning of World War II, it had dropped to 96 percent. By the Korean War, only 81 percent of men tested had sufficient reading skills to function as a soldier. By the end of Viet Nam in 1973, the literacy rate was down to 73 percent.

With each drop in the ability to read, however, the amount of formal schooling had actually increased. The men with the lowest reading ability were supposedly the best educated. They had been in school the longest.[17] In 1920, 98 percent of those entering military service had adequate reading skills. But only 32 percent of American kids ever went past elementary school.[18] Somehow, they learned to read better without school than later generations did with school.

As school requirements have changed over the past century, the trend has become obvious. Literacy rates have dropped as the amount of schooling has increased. It seems that the more we know, the dumber we get. Forcing our children to memorize facts will not educate them. We have to find ways to stimulate their curiosity and encourage them to reason. Albert Einstein recognized the need for a desire for learning.

> *It is little short of a miracle that modern methods of instruction have not already completely strangled the holy curiosity of inquiry ... I believe that one could even deprive a healthy beast of prey of its voraciousness if one could force it with a whip to eat continuously whether it were hungry or not. (Albert Einstein)*

Apathetic America

There is a constant effort by many people to gain power by bringing a kind of forced conformity to society. It is often subtle and is usually presented to us as a good thing for all of us. A system of education that forces all children to learn certain basic skills seems like a good thing. But it becomes dangerous if we lose the ability to think and just become happy with our allotted place. It becomes dangerous because we do not see the more subtle erosions of freedom.

One of the things that made America such a unique experiment in government was the focus on the rights of the individual. We will examine those rights in more detail in later chapters, but to protect those rights, we have to be educated. Otherwise we become easily swayed by the shallow one-liners and sound bites that have become the staple of political campaigns. If we all learned to reason effectively, then we would no longer be subject to the tremendous influences of television and film. We would actually examine what a political candidate stood for and vote on the content of the person's character and beliefs, rather than on the image that we see on the screen.

Complacency is one of the most dangerous enemies of a free society. It makes us lazy. It makes us willing to hand responsibility to any dictator that promises to take care of us. It makes us sit down and stop thinking. That is the fastest means to slavery. We must absolutely keep our minds active. We must constantly ask questions and learn. We must never stop thinking. Curiosity and a desire for truth and wisdom are not just nice to have. They are requirements for a good citizen.

The need for true education is a deeply spiritual thing as well. When Christians talk of raising their children in the way that they should go, it does not mean teaching them to blindly follow a list of commandments so that they will be good boys and girls. Rather it means that we, as parents, are responsible to teach our children the principles of scripture and teach them to think in such a way that they can discern right from wrong on their own. Just following rules is a lazy way out. We have to teach our children to desire wisdom.

Of course that requires that we be something more than just robots ourselves.

Intelligence appears to be the thing that enables a man to get along without education. Education enables a man to get along without the use of his intelligence. (Albert Edward Wiggam)

When we talk about the responsibilities that we have as citizens, this need to be educated cannot be ignored. It is absolutely imperative that we take the time to learn to think. Harry V. Jaffa describes the United States Constitution as a "bundle of compromises."[19] It is necessary to be able to read the Constitution and discern the difference between the compromises and the principles. Otherwise we apply laws where they were never intended to be applied and use the law as a weapon to keep people in subjection rather than as a protection of their freedom. Our Founding Fathers focused on individuals. Tyranny focuses on the state.

The struggle that we face is a war for the minds of Americans. If we do not learn to think, to reason, to analyze and to use our minds, in short, to be educated, then we are not true to the vision of the Founding Fathers.

But what do we mean by the American Revolution? Do we mean the American war? The Revolution was effected before the war commenced. The Revolution was in the minds and hearts of the people; a change in their religious sentiments of their duties and obligations . . . This radical change in the principles, opinions, sentiments, and affections of the people was the real American Revolution. (John Adams)

[1] Bowen, *Miracle at Philadelphia*, pg. 4.

[2] Quoted in Gaustad, *Neither King nor Prelate*, pg. 85.

[3] Royster, *The Destructive War*, pg. 87-88.

[4] Quoted in Royster, *The Destructive War*, pg. 87.

[5] *Ibid.* , pg. 375.

[6] *Ibid.*, pg. 135.

[7] *Ibid.*, pg. 137.

[8] Woodrow Wilson, quoted in Gatto, *The Underground History of American Education*, pg. 38.

[9] *Ibid.*

[10] *Ibid.*

[11] *Ibid.*, pg. 177.

[12] *Ibid.*

[13] *Ibid.*, pg. 224.

[14] *Ibid.*, pg. 45.

[15] *Ibid.*, pg. 106.

[16] Nosworthy, *The Anatomy of Victory*, pg.160.

[17] Gatto, *The Underground History of American Education*, pg. 52.

[18] *Ibid.*, pg. 132)

[19] Jaffa, *Original Intent and the Framers of the Constitution*, pg. 21.

★★★★★

Individual Right #4:

The Right To Enjoyment Of Family

★★★★★

Responsibility #4:

Protect The Sanctity Of The Family

★★★★★

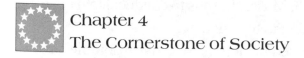 Chapter 4
The Cornerstone of Society

Nor is it true that as soon as a Man weds, his expected Bliss dissolves into slavish Cares and Bondage. . . . as to the Cares, they are chiefly what attend the bringing up of Children; and I would ask any Man who has experienced it, if they are not the most delightful Cares in the World; and if from that Particular alone, he does not find the Bliss of a double State much greater, instead of being less than he expected. (Benjamin Franklin, 1734)

George Washington once remarked that until there is a new order of things, men and women will experience passionate yearnings for each other.[1] He might have been thinking of the courtship and marriage of John Adams and Abigail Smith. They exchanged over 1,100 letters between 1762 and the end of Adams' political career in 1801. The earliest were filled with romantic allusions that probably don't sound to modern readers like they could come out of Puritan Massachusetts.

Abigail was the daughter of a minister. John met her when she was fifteen years old. He wasn't that impressed at the time but a couple of years later he changed his mind. He said then that she was "a constant feast. Tender, feeling, sensible, friendly. A friend. Not an imprudent, not an indelicate, not a disagreeable word or action. Prudent, modest, delicate, soft, sensible, obliging, active." He began riding four miles to Weymouth, Massachusetts to conduct legal business by day and court Abigail by night.[2]

John addressed his letters to "Miss Adorable" and to "Diana," referring to the Roman goddess of purity and love. He was ardent and passionate.

> *Miss Adorable*
>
> *By the same Token that the Bearer hereof satt up with you last night I hereby order you to give him, as many Kisses, and as many Hours of your Company after 9 O'Clock as he shall please to Demand and charge them to my Account: This Order, or Requisition call it which you will is in Consideration of a similar order Upon Aurelia for the like favour, and I presume I have good Right to draw upon you for the Kisses as I have given two or three Millions at least, when one has been received, and of Consequence the Account between us is immensely in favour of yours,*
>
> *John Adams*

Her letters were equally ardent. It was a romance remarked on by most who knew them. But courtship was a little different in those days. It's not that we do not consider marriage and family unimportant now. We do. But there have been forces at work for the past hundred years that have tried to alter how we view family. The changes in our educational system that we discussed in the last chapter have taken their toll. We need to look at them carefully so that we do not lose the sanctity of family.

Family in Early America

There was a time in New England when it was considered so important for people to be in families that the legal system took steps to insure that everyone was. The provinces of Connecticut and Plymouth passed laws that made it illegal for a single person to live alone.[3] And they were not idle laws. The records indicate that in 1668, in Middlesex County, Massachusetts, the court searched the town for single people and placed them in families. A man named John Littleale in Essex County apparently resisted being forced to give up his solitude in 1672. The court noted:

> *Being informed that John Littleale of Haverhill lay in a house by himself contrary to the law of the country, whereby he is subject to much sin and iniquity, which ordinarily are the companions and consequences of a solitary life, it was ordered . . . he remove and settle himself in some orderly family in the town, and be subject to the orderly rules of family government.*[4]

Littleale was given six weeks to comply or he would be thrown in jail. Order in the family was of paramount importance to the Puritans. In Massachusetts, the selectmen and constables of each town were required to periodically inspect families to make sure they maintained "good order." If the family fell into disorder, they were to remove the children and put them in families where there was order.[5]

The Quakers of Pennsylvania believed that the primary role of the family was to raise its children and to promote the spiritual health of its members.[6] In the backcountry of Virginia, honor and shame were so closely tied to family that a person who lost honor brought shame on the entire family.[7] The biblical view made family one of the most important things in all of creation. In God's eyes, a family is the cure for loneliness.

> *God sets the solitary in families.*
> (Psalm 68:6)

This does not mean that the society was perfect. There were plenty of problems. Children rebelled then just like they do now. In the years leading up to the Revolutionary War, premarital pregnancy was an increasing problem. Birth records in Massachusetts show a growing percentage of new mothers giving birth less than nine months after the marriage. In the 1740s, 19 percent of firstborn children were conceived out of wedlock. In the next decade the number grew to 26 percent and by 1774, just two years before the Declaration of Independence, 41 percent of firstborn children were conceived before marriage.[8] It was not a simple matter of youthful lust. In an age when marriage was not allowed without parental consent, many young people forced their parents to give consent in order to avoid the family shame of an unmarried daughter being pregnant. Rebellion against parents is not new.

★★★★★

Without family, a person had no stability in life and no real standing in the community.

★★★★★

What was different in early America was the degree to which family ties remained strong, even when the children rebelled. They never got too far away. Without family, a person had no stability in life and no real standing in the community. Family was everything. It was not an end in itself. It was an instrument of God.[9] Children did not rebel to get out of the family. They rebelled to gain the freedom to start their own. There was never a time in American history when the family was not considered the most basic element of society and the protection of hearth and home have always been the most compelling reason for any action.

Loss of the Family

Anthropologist Margaret Mead commented on the enduring quality of the family unit: "No matter how many communes anybody invents, the family always creeps back." All of history proves that the family unit is indispensable.

Yet there have always been those who have tried to undermine the influence of the family. Dictators such as Hitler made the State more important than the family and tried to impose a regimented instruction that would draw the allegiance of children away from their parents and transfer it to the nation. The Hitler Youth were just one example. For tyranny to succeed, the government must control the thinking of the people. No one can be allowed to think independently. The best way to do that is to force the children into a regimented school system that is designed to teach obedience rather than thought and to separate children from the influences of their parents and family.

Every dictator has set out to accomplish this goal and the inevitable means used is regimented schooling that indoctrinates its students. The breakdown of family cohesion is the first indication that society has lost its godliness. Jesus described family members turning on each other as a sign of the end times.

You will be betrayed even by parents and brothers, relatives and friends. (Luke 21:16)

This pattern describes the direction of the education system of the United States since the Civil War. The only difference is that the tyrant in America is not a single person. It is industrialization itself. But the goal, as we saw in the last chapter, is still the control of people's thoughts.

To accomplish these goals, educators recognized that the family had to be restructured so that society or the State became more important than parents. The school system had to replace the family. This may seem like an extreme view but the educators of America have declared openly for 150 years that this is their goal. We have just not paid much attention.

In 1840, a group called the Massachusetts School Committee began discussing the deterioration of family life as America changed from an agricultural society to an industrial nation. The noted Massachusetts educationalist, Horace Mann, often chaired those meetings. What Mann recognized was that industrialization created "artificial wants." People became increasingly interested in the collection of things. Gradually they lost any ability to be satisfied outside of the excitement of mechanical entertainment. Mann believed that the trend from agricultural life to urbanization meant the end of the family as it used to be. Fathers were diverted from the training of their children by the rigors of industrial work. Because working in a factory kept him away from his children for so much of the day, he was considered to be no longer qualified to teach proper values to his family.[10]

The solution was to separate the child from the family, at least in a social sense. The drive to make good workers for the factories by changing the educational system also meant breaking up the influence of the family. Scholars were able to quote philosophers and theologians such as Plato, Augustine, Erasmus, Luther, Calvin, Hobbes and Rousseau to prove that without compulsory universal schooling, the family would never give up its influence on children. The family had to be discouraged from teaching children to be self-sufficient. Children needed to be indoctrinated into the greater good, the welfare of the state.[11]

Mann declared that the State should be the primary parent of the child. If the parents failed, then the State should step in to fill the parent's place.[12] As we saw, Massachusetts always had laws that allowed the government to step in when the order in a family broke down. With the new direction, however, the State began to change the criteria for determining when a breakdown occurred. Before, a breakdown was defined as something that constituted a threat to the child's health and well-being. Now it was a threat to the child's adherence to new school standards. In this context, the opinion of Justice Paige in the 1840 case *Mercein v People* is ominous.

> *The moment a child is born it owes allegiance to the government of the country of its birth, and is entitled to the protection of the government.*[13]

The child owes allegiance to the State. The State owes protection to the child. But protection against what? It used to be child abuse. Now it is protection from the wrong values taught in the family setting of early America. Boston school superintendent, John Philbrick, said in 1863, regarding the school, "Here is real home!"[14]

The National Education Association (NEA) was founded in 1857. Its mission statement indicates a commitment to quality education.

> *NEA believes every child in America, regardless of family income or place of residence, deserves a quality education. In pursuing its mission, NEA has determined that it will focus the energy and resources of its 2.7 million members on improving the quality of teaching, increasing student achievement and making schools safer, better places to learn.*

What this means to the family is perhaps indicated by the words of Catherine Barrett, NEA president in 1973.

> *Dramatic changes in the way we raise our children are indicated, particularly in terms of schooling. . . we will be agents of change.*

Those changes began much earlier, of course. The NEA's policy document, put out in 1918, called *Cardinal Principles*, announced a dumbed-down curriculum that lowered the standards for students while giving the appearance of doing something good for the child.[15]

We have barely scratched the surface of this subject. But we believe it to be important, first because it has made the average American forget how to reason, but also, we believe that the methods of education today have had a detrimental effect on the family.

Extended Childhood

What is the purpose of school? Dr. Jay Klusky, author of *Easy A's: Winning the School Game*, answers that question in regard to high school.

> *First and foremost the purpose of high school is to learn how to work. The vast majority of students begin their freshman year as old children. We want them to graduate as young adults.*

He then goes on to explain the difference between children and adults.

> *Children play first, adults work first. While this is not the only difference, it is a very important one. . . . Most parents and teachers I talk with seem to put more stock in effort than in grades.*

Klusky's comments highlight what we think is the problem of our educational system. In high school, our children are still "old children." In early America, they would have been considered young adults. Benjamin Franklin was working by the time he was a teenager. So were George Washington and Thomas Edison. For some reason, we no longer think them capable of such responsibility.

One of the effects of forced schooling has been an extension of the number of years that children remain children. The chief purpose of the Education Trust that we referred to earlier, in the words of Benjamin Kidd, was to "impose on the young the ideal of subordination."[16] This was done by requiring children to stay in school for a longer period of time so that they would remain dependent for a longer time. In the words of John Taylor Gatto:

> *Forced schooling was the medicine to bring the whole continental population into conformity with these plans so it might be regarded as a "human resource." Managed as a "workforce." No more Ben Franklins or Tom Edisons could be allowed; they set a bad example. One way to manage this transformation was to see to it that individuals were prevented from taking up their working lives until an advanced age when the ardor of youth and its insufferable self-confidence had cooled.*[17]

Ellwood P. Cubberley, in *Public Education in the United States*, in 1934, declared that "It has become desirable that children should not engage in productive labor." In a section titled "A New Lengthening of the Period of Dependence," he explained that the new factory system made extended childhood necessary by depriving children of the training and education that farm and village life used to give them. As a result of what he called the "all conquering march of machinery," we now had an army of workers who knew nothing.[18]

People used to be either children or adults. Today we have added a third category called teenagers. The teenager didn't exist in any other culture. Most societies in history have had some form of a rite of passage. In primitive tribes, it is often a ritual that involves the young man submitting himself to a painful test that allows him to prove that he is a man. The

Jewish ritual of *Bar Mitzvah* is just such a coming of age rite. Most rites of this nature are done around the age of twelve. They have always been society's way of saying that the child is now an adult.

Cultures with a rite of manhood rarely have any problems with juvenile delinquency. When you are a child, you are treated as a child. When a child misbehaves, he is disciplined. But the personal responsibility is limited. Once you become an adult, you are responsible for

People used to be either children or adults. Today we have added a third category called teenagers.

your behavior. And if you violate the standards of society after that, you are either executed or banished.

Modern America has no rite of manhood. There is no clear transition from childhood to adult life. Through our system of education, we have encouraged our children to believe that they are not personally responsible for anything. By the time they leave school and enter the workforce, they are not educated enough to do much of anything but get a job working for someone else and trudge through life seeking entertainment on the weekends. They have learned to be selfish.

It is the family that has suffered from all of this. We want to suggest a few things to parents. Regardless of what school a child goes to, whether public, private, religious or whatever, it is not the school's responsibility to teach values. It is not the school's business to teach moral judgment. The school system has come to believe that it has the right to teach those things. And most parents have come to expect the school to teach those things. We understand that most educators honestly and sincerely believe these principles. And with so many parents failing to take their responsibilities as parents, it is not hard to understand how they arrived at those beliefs. But the truth is that it is the parents who are responsible.

> *Train up a child in the way he should go,*
> *And when he is old he will not depart from it.*
> (Proverbs 22:6)

Parents need to also remember that whatever one hears first is what he is inclined to believe. Once the belief is there, it is very difficult to change. It takes an ounce of information to form a perception and a ton of information to change it. Therefore, if the school trains a child with wrong perceptions, beliefs and values, it will take a tremendous effort to correct. It is imperative that parents be the first ones to instill perceptions into their children, while they are still young and still at home. We dare not wait until they are in school.

As citizens of the United States of America, we have a responsibility to train our children so that they can make good decisions no matter where they are. If we as parents have given that training in the home, if we have placed the integrity of family in its proper place of priority, if we have acted as the priests and the protectors of our homes and families, then we will never need to fear the influences of society. It will not matter what a teacher says. If it is contrary to biblical values, our children will have the capacity to analyze it and reject it.

If we ever lose the sanctity of family, then we will also lose our individual rights and freedoms as Americans. To maintain the sanctity of the family, we must first educate ourselves and then teach our children. What should we teach them?

> *Children should be educated and instructed in the principles of freedom.* (John Adams)

---

[1] Quoted in Bennet, *Our Sacred Honor*, pg. 106.

[2] *Ibid.*, pg. 105.

[3] Fischer, *Albion's Seed*, pg. 73.

[4] *Ibid.*

[5] *Ibid.*, pg. 72.

[6] *Ibid.*, pg. 484.

[7] *Ibid.*, pg. 668.

[8] Gross, *The Minutemen and Their World*, pg. 217.

[9] Fischer, *Albion's Seed*, pg. 68.

[10] Gatto, *The Underground History of American Education*, pg. 119.

[11] *Ibid.*

[12] *Ibid.*

[13] *Ibid.*, pg. 120.

[14] *Ibid.*, pg. 124.

[15] *Ibid.*, pg. 109.

[16] *Ibid.*, pg. 38.

[17] *Ibid.*

[18] *Ibid.*, pg. 39.

★★★★★

Individual Right #5

The Right to Equality

★★★★★

Responsibility #5

Recognize The Equality Of All People

★★★★★

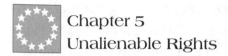

The end of government being the good of mankind points out its great duties: it is above all things to provide for the security, the quiet, and happy enjoyment of life, liberty, and property.
(James Otis)

Ask a group of people to name the first great American hero in the struggle for independence and it will be a rare occurrence if anyone mentions the name James Otis. He is one of the least known important figures in American history. Yet he was one of the most notable leaders in the years before the break with Great Britain. If he was not the first American hero of that war, then he was certainly among the first. He was definately the first to attract the focused hostility of the British government.

Otis was a lawyer. He graduated from Harvard and practiced in Plymouth for a short time before moving to Boston. He began to draw much attention to himself as a capable attorney and was appointed to the very important position of the King's Advocate General of the vice-admiralty court in Boston. But his real reputation came when he resigned in order to oppose the government over a controversial case involving "Writs of Assistance."

The real conflict between Britain and America started with the world-wide struggle between France and Britain called the Seven Years War, known in America as the French and Indian War. At the time, France controlled Canada, and England controlled America. It was a long and very costly war for Britain but the American phase ended in 1760 when Canada fell and the British forces took charge. The French threat was ended.

During the war, many American colonists carried on a very lucrative – and illegal – trade with the French West Indies. Smuggling became such a profitable enterprise that New Englanders looked on it as a respectable business, so much so that British attempts to put a stop to it were extremely unpopular.

The British, for their part, saw smuggling as more than just trading with the enemy. They saw immense amounts of tax revenue being lost. At the same time, they were trying to figure out how to recoup their losses from the war. They determined to end smuggling and, at the same time, find a way to get the colonists to help pay for the thousands of British troops who were stationed in America for the protection of the colonists from both the French and the Indians along the frontier.

The problem with arresting smugglers, however, was that it was difficult to collect enough evidence to piece together a valid case. Authorities with experience in fighting smuggling proposed a law that would enable them to issue general search warrants that allowed them to search whatever premises they chose any time they wanted. They were called Writs of Assistance and they were very unpopular, but they proved to be very effective.

Writs were issued for the life of the monarch plus six months, so when the king died in 1760, a new application was presented to the Superior Court of Massachusetts. The government's agent appointed to argue in their favor was James Otis.

Otis was a man of principle. He was convinced that the Writs of Assistance were a violation of the individual rights of citizens and, rather than argue for their issuance, he resigned his post and represented a group of merchantmen who were opposed to them. He stood in court and presented a nearly five-hour speech that became the basis of colonial resistance over the next two decades. John Adams later said, "In that Boston courtroom, American independence was there and then born."[1]

Otis later wrote a series of pamphlets that explained his position in more detail. In particular, one called "the Rights of the British Colonies Asserted and Proved" was widely read. His opposition to the government cost him dearly in the long run. His wife was a staunch loyalist and the more he sided with the colonists, the more his marriage deteriorated. In 1769, he got into a brawl with a loyalist and suffered a severe head injury. He was never the same mentally after that and had to withdraw from public life. He died in 1783 when he was struck by lightning.

Because Otis' career did not last into the crucial years of the Revolution, few Americans today are familiar with his name. To the Founding Fathers, however, he was a hero. He was greatly respected by everyone, even his enemies. His constant nemesis, Thomas Hutchinson, governor of Massachusetts, the most consistent political opponent that Otis faced, portrayed him as a man who never took advantage of inadvertent or minor points such as clerical errors. Instead, when in the courtroom or in political assemblies, he argued from the basis of principle.[2] He set forth the philosophical foundation for all that was to follow. The principles that he elaborated are echoed in the Declaration of Independence and any American who does not understand them has no real understanding of his heritage.

The Declaration of Independence

Thomas Jefferson once composed an inscription for his tombstone. It listed the three things for which he most wanted to be remembered. The first thing on the list was the Declaration of Independence. He was understandably proud of it. It was the birth certificate of the country. Everything that is the United States of America is dated from that document. Before the Declaration, there were thirteen colonies. After it, there was a nation.

The time was June of 1776. The colonies had been in a virtual state of war for some time already. British troops had closed Boston in order to teach the malcontents a lesson. There was no trade going in or out. For a merchant center and a port, that meant financial ruin. Soldiers had marched inland to destroy stores of weapons and ammunition reported to be hidden at Concord by the rebels. The resulting clash with a rag tag collection of militia at Lexington turned a tense political situation into violence. The British completed their work with ruthless efficiency, at least as much as they could. The colonists had already moved most of the arms.

★★★★★

Before the Declaration, there were thirteen colonies. After it, there was a nation.

★★★★★

They then set out to return the way they came. The colonists skirmished with the British all the way back to Boston and established siege lines around the city. Eventually the battle of Bunker Hill followed.

In Philadelphia, representatives from each of the thirteen colonies had been gathered to form some sort of unified political action. Months before, they had sent a list of grievances to the King of England in the hope that bloodshed could be avoided. Spring became summer and there was no response. The escalating violence demanded some sort of decision.

It came in the form of a resolution introduced on June 7 by Richard Henry Lee of Virginia.

> *Resolved: That these United Colonies are, and of right ought to be, free and independent states, that they are absolved from all allegiance to the British Crown, and that all political connection between them and the State of Great Britain is, and ought to be, totally dissolved.*

The Lee Resolution was discussed for some time. Most were not quite ready to make a complete break with the mother country. But it looked increasingly as though there would be no other choice. So a five-man committee was appointed to draft a statement of the colonies' case to be presented to the world if the vote for independence should pass.

Jefferson was a member of that committee, representing the colony of Virginia. Also appointed were John Adams from Massachusetts, Roger Sherman of Connecticut, Benjamin Franklin of Pennsylvania and Robert R. Livingston from New York.

The committee discussed what they would write and voted to have Adams and Jefferson create the first draft. Adams later recalled his first meeting with Jefferson.

The subcommittee met. Jefferson proposed to me to make the draft. I said, "I will not." "You should do it." "Oh! no." "Why will you not? You ought to do it." "I will not." "Why?" "Reasons enough." "What can be your reasons?" "Reason first, you are a Virginian, and a Virginian ought to appear at the head of this business. Reason second, I am obnoxious, suspected, and unpopular. You are very much otherwise. Reason third, you can write ten times better than I can." "Well," said Jefferson, "if you are decided, I will do as well as I can." "Very well, when you have drawn it up, we will have a meeting."

When the Continental Congress reconvened on July 1, the Lee Resolution was taken up again and the next day it was adopted by twelve of the thirteen colonies with New York not voting. That state added its approval a few days later to make it unanimous.

The Declaration was discussed for the following two days and, with a few revisions, approved in the late afternoon of July 4, 1776. We actually celebrate America's beginning on the day that the Declaration was approved rather than July 2, the day that independence was approved.

A good quality copy was made and the delegates gathered to sign it, though not until a month later, on August 2. Some were not present then and had to sign it later. A few never signed it at all. But the step was taken and the colonies were united in a monumental undertaking.

Adams, in a letter to Timothy Pickering in 1822, recalled the substance of the Declaration.

As you justly observe, there is not an idea in it but what had been hackneyed in Congress for two years before. The substance of it is contained in the declaration of rights and the violation of those rights in the Journals of Congress in 1774. Indeed, the essence of it is contained in a pamphlet, voted and printed by the town of Boston, before the first congress met, composed by James Otis, as I suppose, in one of his lucid intervals, and pruned and polished by Samuel Adams.

It was not new in concept, but it was something that had never actually been tried before. It was certainly important. In 1825, Jefferson called it "an expression of the American mind."[3] He and James Madison, the father of the Constitution, were asked to make a list of books and documents that should be read by law students at the new University of Virginia so that they would gain a solid foundation in the principles of American law and government. They proposed first and foremost "the Declaration of Independence as the fundamental act of Union of these States."[4] The Constitution became the framework of American government but the Declaration explained the heart and soul of it. In the words of Harry Jaffa:

As the "fundamental act of Union" the Declaration was and remains the fundamental legal instrument attesting to the existence of the United States. From it all subsequent acts of the people of the United States, including the Constitution, are dated and authorized. It defines at once the legal and the moral personality of that "one People" (who are also said to be a "good people") who separated themselves from Great Britain and became free and independent. It thereby also defines the source and nature of that authority which is involved when "We the people of the Untied States" ordained and established the Constitution. For the same principle of authority—that of the people—that made the independence of the states lawful, made lawful all the acts and things done subsequently in their name. This tells us why the Constitution ought to be obeyed, why we have a duty to obey it, why and in what sense it may be truly said that the voice of the people is the voice of God. For these reasons the Declaration remains the most fundamental dimension of the law of the Constitution.[5]

The Constitution of the United States is the law of this land but the Declaration is the mission statement. It is thus sad that Americans are so dreadfully unfamiliar with the principles that it describes. We need to learn them. We have included it in its entirety in Appendix I. For now, we will focus on the preamble. The whole philosophical basis of America's existence is explained in a few lines.

When in the Course of human events, it becomes necessary for one people to dissolve the political bands which have connected them with another, and to assume among the powers of the earth, the separate and equal station to which the

Laws of Nature and of Nature's God entitle them, a decent respect to the opinions of mankind requires that they should declare the causes which impel them to the separation.

We hold these truths to be self-evident, that all men are created equal, that they are endowed by their Creator with certain unalienable Rights, that among these are Life, Liberty and the pursuit of Happiness, – That to secure these rights, Governments are instituted among Men, deriving their just powers from the consent of the governed, – That whenever any Form of government becomes destructive of these ends, it is the Right of the People to alter or to abolish it, and to institute new Government, laying its foundation on such principles and organizing its powers in such form, as to them shall seem most likely to effect their Safety and Happiness.

The Right To Equality

We should start with the self-evident truth that all men are created equal. The history of humanity demonstrates that it is apparently not all that self-evident. Virtually every society and culture that we have knowledge of has had some kind of caste structure. We mentioned the Hindu castes in the last chapter. It is blatantly structured and easy to see but other cultures have had the same kind of problem.

Even America has some degree of social status but it is remarkably different than other cultures. Americans have the basic belief that anyone can ascend from the lowest level of society to the highest through hard work and perseverance.

America is the home of the rags to riches story. It is this aspect of equality that made the American experiment so unique. In America you are what you make of yourself. If you want to work, you can succeed. The inequality of America is produced by the efforts of the individual. Educator Felix E. Schelling expressed it this way:

> *True education makes for inequality; the inequality of individuality, the inequality of success, the glorious inequality of talent, of genius.*

All of this is possible because in America, the rights of the individual have been given such importance. We talk about patriotism in terms of service to the country. John F. Kennedy's immortal words from his 1961 Inaugural Address stir us all.

> *And so, my fellow Americans: ask not what your country can do for you – ask what you can do for your country.*

In most nations, patriotism is founded on a loyalty to the land and to the history of the nation or to the religion of the culture. In America, it is more to an idea. To be an American does not indicate any particular racial background. Rather, it includes virtually every race and nationality in the world.

Dinesh D'Souza, in his book *What's So Great About America*, points out that a person can "become" an American, something that has no parallel in other countries.[6] If a German comes to America, he can become an American, but an

American going to Germany will not become a German. He might take on German citizenship, but he will not "become" German. Someone moving from India to America can "become" an American, but a person moving from America to India will not "become" Indian. America is not a racial identification. It is a loyalty to an ideal.

This does not mean that the ideal is completely achieved. Slavery certainly constituted a racial bias and we still deal with vestiges of that racism. But even then, those who came out of slavery recognized that the concept of freedom should be available to everyone, regardless of race. Dr. Martin Luther King expressed that hope eloquently in his famous "I Have a Dream" speech.

> *I say to you today, my friends, that in spite of the difficulties and frustrations of the moment, I still have a dream. It is a dream deeply rooted in the American dream. I have a dream that one day this nation will rise up and live out the true meaning of its creed: "We hold these truths to be self-evident: that all men are created equal."*

To be an American is to adhere to an ideal. And that ideal was expressed in the very first official document of the United States: "All men are created equal."

Philosophical Foundations

The founders of the United States were men who were well versed in political and legal philosophy. They knew the history of various forms of government and the strengths and weaknesses of those governments. They were educated on the books of several men who had far reaching influence on the design of American government. The names of the authors of those books should be familiar to every American but sadly are not. Four in particular deserve at least passing attention – John Locke, Charles de Montesquieu, Emmerich de Vattel and William Blackstone. It was primarily from their writings that the Declaration of Independence and the Constitution were inspired. They were all concerned with the rights of mankind and the form that government should take to protect those rights.

★★★★★

The basic individual rights of life, liberty and property existed in a state of nature.

★★★★★

Locke was the earliest. He was a British philosopher who wrote on a variety of subjects, including *A Letter on Toleration*, which we will refer to later when we discuss the separation of church and state. In 1690, Locke published a treatise called *An Essay Concerning the True Original Extent and End of Civil Government*. In it, he outlined the basis for the rights of every individual.

Locke traced the development of rights from the earliest state of mankind. He called it a "state of nature." In that state, every man had certain inherent rights, which Locke identified as the right to life, liberty and property. In that state, every man is independent of every other. If someone tries to deprive him of his rights, he is justified in resisting to protect his interests. The possession of these basic rights was a "law of nature" and did not depend on government.

The problem with the state of nature is that someone who is stronger can violate the rights of others through brute force. The solution was for several people to band together for their own mutual protection. A group had more strength than any individual. They formed what Locke called a "social compact." Basically that meant that they agreed to give up a small part of their freedom in return for the benefits of joint action.

Locke believed that all government was based on the social compact, a concept that was expressed in the Declaration of Independence as "consent of the governed." The phrase "social compact" appeared frequently in the conversations of the Founding Fathers. James Madison repeatedly declared that "all power in just and free government is derived from compact."[7]

Regardless of the type of government, however, Locke wrote that the basic individual rights of life, liberty and property existed in a state of nature and could not be legally taken away from anyone. They belonged to the individual simply because he was human. Anytime a government attempted to violate those rights, Locke declared that the people had a right to change the government, even if that required violent revolution.

The next philosopher to have a great impact on early America was a French writer named Charles de Montesquieu. He extended the idea of individual rights to the responsibility of government. With Locke, he believed that the purpose of government was to protect the rights of man. He proposed a separation of powers within the government so that no one branch could become too strong and impose its will on the others and on the people. Montesquieu's concepts became the basic structure of American government, with the Administrative branch represented by the President, the

Legislative branch in the Congress and the Judicial branch in the Supreme Court. Each was given the power to check the other two. We must not lose sight of the fact that this very workable system was intended primarily to protect the individual.

Emmerich de Vattel, while not in agreement with much of what Locke believed, nevertheless expounded the idea of individual rights. He wrote what he considered to be the ideal structure of government in a book called *The Law of Nations*, published in 1759 and widely read in America. Many of the discussions in the Constitutional Convention involved Vattel's work. Benjamin Franklin, for example, received a copy as a gift from Charles Dumas and remarked in a thank you letter that it "has been continually in the hands of members of our congress, now sitting."

Vattel recognized that human beings were not really independent of each other. They are social creatures and they need each other.

> *Man is so formed by nature, that he cannot supply all his own wants, but necessarily stands in need of the intercourse and assistance of his fellow-creatures, whether for his immediate preservation, or for the sake of perfecting his nature, and enjoying such a life as is suitable to a rational being.*

For Vattel, the state of nature was the natural association of human beings with each other for the betterment of the whole society. The purpose of government was to insure the protection of life for the people, to protect them from outside interference with their rights and to procure their happiness, which Vattel defined as developing their potential for growth toward perfection. The phrase in the Declaration of Independence "pursuit of happiness" can probably be traced to Vattel more than anyone else. Like Locke and Montesquieu, Vattel believed that the violation of individual rights resulted in justification for rebellion.

Between 1765 and 1769, William Blackstone published a series of lectures under the title *Commentaries on the Laws of England*. They became the basic law texts for the American legal system until well after the Civil War. Blackstone further expounded on the

> Vattel recognized that human beings were not really independent of each other.

concept of separation of powers with the intention of protecting the natural rights of all men under the "laws of nature."

All of these men, and our Founding Fathers from James Otis to John Adams and Thomas Jefferson, understood the most fundamental element of American liberty to be the protection of the rights of the individual and that every human being had the same claim to those rights. They are "unalienable," meaning that we cannot be alienated from them. They cannot be taken away. Any attempt to remove them is equivalent to slavery.

By being or becoming members of society
they have not renounced their natural liberty in

any greater degree than other good citizens, and
if tis taken from them without their consent they
are so far enslaved. (James Otis)

Bad governments may repress rights and prevent people from enjoying them, but they cannot remove them. The very beginning of independence in America was built on that immortal and self-evident phrase.

All men are created equal.

The Dred Scott Case

Dred Scott was a slave in the early 1800s. His owner died in 1832 and he was sold to an army surgeon named Dr. John Emerson. Emerson moved with Scott to the free state of Illinois in 1836 for two and a half years, then to a fort in Wisconsin. The time that was spent in Illinois gave Scott the right to make a claim for freedom but he never did, possibly because he did not know that he could. Two years after moving to Wisconsin, Emerson was transferred to the south. He was there for a year before he sent for Scott to join him.

Scott and his family (he was allowed to marry another slave and Emerson purchased her so they could be together) traveled to meet Emerson, who died in 1843. Emerson's widow hired Scott out to an army captain, which prompted Scott to sue for his freedom, claiming rights that extended back to his time in Illinois.

The case became infamous in the national news. After ten years of appeals and retrials, it eventually came to the Supreme Court. Seven of the nine justices were supporters of slavery and their bias showed in the decision that the court reached.

The majority decision, given by Chief Justice Roger B. Taney, centered on the question of whether or not Scott could be a citizen. Ultimately he declared that Scott was in fact merely property and could not legally bring a lawsuit. Therefore he had to remain a slave.

In making this statement, Taney appealed to the words of the Declaration of Independence.

The legislation and histories of the times, and the language used in the Declaration of Independence, show, that neither the class of persons who had been imported as slaves, nor their descendants, whether they had become free or not, were then acknowledged as a part of the people, nor intended to be included in the general words used in that memorable instrument.

In referring to the "legislation and histories of the times," Taney implied that, if the Founding Fathers intended to include the slaves in the population to whom the rights of the Declaration of Independence extended, they would have immediately outlawed slavery. Because they didn't, they must have meant to exclude those of African descent from ever being citizens of the United States and therefore slaves had no rights whatsoever. Taney actually quoted from the Declaration and then insisted that it justified restricting the rights of Dred Scott.

The language of the Declaration of Independence is equally Conclusive: .. .

We hold these truths to be self-evident: that all men are created equal; that they are endowed by their Creator with certain unalienable rights; that among them is life, liberty, and the pursuit of happiness; that to secure these rights, Governments are instituted, deriving their just powers from the consent of the governed.

The general word above quoted would seem to embrace the whole human family, and if they were used in a similar instrument at this day would be so understood. But it is too clear for dispute, that the enslaved African race were not intended to be included, and formed no part of the people who framed and adopted this declaration; for if the language, as understood in that day, would embrace them, the conduct of the distinguished men who framed the Declaration of Independence would have been utterly and flagrantly inconsistent with the principles they asserted; and instead of the sympathy of mankind, to which they so confidently appeared, they would have deserved and received universal rebuke and reprobation.

The court's decision was that because Scott was black he was not a citizen and therefore he had no rights and could not sue. He was therefore kept in slavery.

Many, especially in the South, accepted the logic of Taney's argument. Others were outraged. Among them was Abraham Lincoln. He recognized that the Founding Fathers knew America was not perfect and that they provided for America to grow toward the goal of equality.

Many of the Founding Fathers, including Jefferson and Washington, owned slaves. But they also recognized that there was a fundamental problem inherent in a system that robbed men, regardless of color, of their freedoms. Washington provided for the release of all of his slaves at his death. Jefferson, in his *Notes on Virginia*, attacked the practice of slavery. They were faced with the dilemma of how to bring about an end to slavery in a way that would not leave the uneducated slaves worse off than before.

Lincoln recognized that the opinions of society were strongly pro-slavery in early America and that to press too strongly for an end to slavery would have doomed even the possibility of forming the United States. In fact, the issue of slavery was discussed at great length in the

In Lincoln's words, "I would consent to any great evil, to avoid a greater one."

Constitutional Convention. For the most part, it was tabled to be discussed at a later time. Jefferson's original draft of the Declaration of Independence contained statements against slavery. They were all deleted by the other delegates before the document was signed. The whole discussion was put aside so that the more important matter of establishing the nation could be accomplished. In Lincoln's words, "I would consent to any great evil, to avoid a greater one." Lincoln's response to the Dred Scott decision is worth reading.

Chief Justice Taney, in his opinion in the Dred Scott *case, admits that the language of the Declaration is broad enough to include the whole human family, but he and Judge Douglas argue that the authors of that instrument did not intend to include Negroes, by the fact that they did not at once, actually place them on an equality with the whites. Now this grave argument comes to just nothing at all, by the other fact, that they did not at once, or ever afterwards, actually place all white people on an equality with one another . . . They did not mean to assert the obvious untruth, that all were then actually enjoying that equality, nor yet, that they were about to confer it immediately upon them. In fact they had no power to confer such a boon. They meant simply to declare the right, so that the enforcement of it might follow as fast as circumstances should permit. They meant to set up a standard maxim for free society, which could be familiar to all, and revered by all, constantly looked to, constantly labored for, and even though never perfectly attained, constantly approximated, and thereby constantly spreading and deepening its influence and augmenting the happiness and value of life to all people of all colors everywhere.*

The Dred Scott story had a happy ending for Scott and his family. The expenses of the long years of trials were paid by the sons of Peter Blow, the man who originally owned Scott and who sold him to Emerson. Blow's sons had become childhood friends with Scott and supported his efforts throughout those long years. When the Supreme Court decided against Scott's claim, they arranged to purchase both Scott and his wife and then gave them their freedom. The story demonstrates not only that we must constantly strive toward the unalienable freedoms that God gave us, but it also shows the importance of relationships.

Nature's God

The most important aspect of individual rights was the recognition that they do not come from a government. Every man has rights simply because he was created with them. For Thomas Jefferson, it was "the Laws of Nature and of Nature's God." The Declaration stated that the rights of life, liberty and the pursuit of happiness were endowed by the Creator, not the Parliament or the Congress. Individual rights come from God. Virtually every one of the Founders recognized this as a fact. In his pamphlets, James Otis traced the rights of man to God.

> *There can be no prescription old enough to supersede the law of nature and the grant of God Almighty, who has given to all men a natural right to be free.*

Alexander Hamilton concurred.

> *The sacred rights of mankind are not to be rummaged for among old parchments or musty records. They are written, as with a sunbeam, in the whole volume of human nature, by the hand*

of divinity itself, and can never be erased or obscured by mortal power.[8]

It is this sacred aspect of individual rights that we need to keep in mind. In the context of biblical principle, all men are created equal.

> *For the LORD your God is God of gods and Lord of lords, the great God, mighty and awesome, who shows no partiality nor takes a bribe.* (Deuteronomy 10:17)

This is the idea behind Paul's criticism of the Corinthians. They had divisions because those who were wealthy looked down on those who were not.

> *Therefore when you come together in one place, it is not to eat the Lord's Supper. For in eating, each one takes his own supper ahead of others, and one is hungry and another is drunk. What! Do you not have houses to eat and drink in? Or do you despise the church of God and shame those who have nothing?* (1 Corinthians 11:20-22)

Paul made it clear that those who failed to recognize the equality of other people were judging them to be unworthy of salvation.

> *But let a man examine himself, and so let him eat of the bread and drink of the cup. For he who*

eats and drinks in an unworthy manner eats and drinks judgment to himself, not discerning the Lord's body. For this reason many are weak and sick among you, and many sleep. For if we would judge ourselves, we would not be judged. (1 Corinthians 11:28-31)

To judge is to say that we can be saved because we are somehow good enough, but the blood of Jesus is not sufficient to save those who are lower than us. God shows no partiality, however, and if the blood of Jesus is not strong enough to save them, then it is not strong enough to save us either and we invite sickness and even death by our judgment. In God's eyes we are all equal, regardless of race, age, gender or economic status.

James states that partiality is not consistent with love. In fact it is transgression.

If you really fulfill the royal law according to the Scripture, "You shall love your neighbor as yourself," you do well; but if you show partiality, you commit sin, and are convicted by the law as transgressors. (James 2:8-9)

The United States is a nation founded on equality. We have a responsibility to recognize and defend the rights of every other person. That does not leave us room to judge people on the basis of race, gender, economic status, religious belief or anything else. Every person has God-given rights simply because he exists. As with so many matters of liberty, James Otis understood the consequences of not understanding this truth.

It is a clear truth that those who every day barter away other men's liberty will soon care little for their own. (James Otis)

---

[1] Quoted in Andrews and Zarefsky, *American Voices*, pg. 36.
[2] Ridpath, *James Otis The Pre Revolutionist*, pg. 52.
[3] Jaffa, *Original Intent and the Framers of the Constitution*, pg. 44.
[4] *Ibid.*, pg. 22.
[5] *Ibid.*, pg. 22-23)
[6] D'Souza, *What's So Great About America*, pg. 33-35.
[7] Jaffa, *Original Intent and the Framers of the Constitution*, pg. 19.
[8] *Ibid.*, pg. 35.

★★★★★

Individual Right #6

The Right To Life

★★★★★

Responsibility #6

Protect And Choose Life

★★★★★

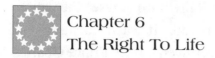

Chapter 6
The Right To Life

The whole secret of a successful life is to find out what it is one's destiny to do, and then do it.
(Henry Ford))

The night of June 16, 1775 saw a flurry of activity on the heights overlooking Charlestown. American militia toiled through the darkness to build a fort that stared threateningly across the harbor at the city of Boston.

With daylight, the occupying British troops in Boston were awakened by the boom of cannon fire from *HMS Lively*, a prelude to the concentrated fire of the entire British squadron in Boston harbor. Once the officers in charge realized the extent of the American fortifications, they set troops in motion toward what would become known as the Battle of Bunker Hill. Until the troops could attack, the cannon pounded the American positions.[1]

The battle would produce many new heroes in the American struggle for Independence, many who are virtually unknown to most modern Americans. Dr. Joseph Warren, for example, whose name was always linked at the time with Samuel Adams and John Hancock, would fall dead in the redoubt later that day, shot in the head at some point near the end of the fight.[2] He was a man who had no ulterior motive in joining the rebels. He could easily have stayed aloof as most other physicians in Boston did, but he simply believed the Americans were right.[3]

The excitable Israel Putnam would display great courage and leadership throughout the day. Though few Americans know his name, his words, "Don't fire until you see the whites of their eyes," are well remembered. It wasn't a statement that was original with him. He borrowed it from Prince Charles of Prussia who said it at the Battle of Jägerndorf in 1745, but that doesn't detract from Putnam's courage or his leadership.[4]

The first real hero of the morning, however, was William Prescott, a tall farmer from Pepperell, Massachusetts. He had seen action in colonial regiments during the French and Indian War. He was known for his cool courage under fire. On this fateful day, he commanded the motley collection of farmers digging away in preparation for the British assault.

The first crisis came when a British cannonball decapitated a man named Asa Pollard. One minute he was standing there and the next minute his head was gone in a shower of blood and flesh. To the young and inexperienced farmers, the barrage of 168 big guns was unnerving enough, but to see a man they all knew killed in such a grisly fashion was almost too much.[5]

Prescott drove them back to work. He ordered them to bury Asa "without prayers" and ignored the group of men who gathered around a chaplain in blatant disregard for his orders. To steady the men, he jumped up on the top of the earthwork and strolled up and down in plain view of the British artillery, shouting, "It was a one in a million shot, men. See how close they come to hitting me!"[6] His men watched in awe as the British ships took aim at him in hopes of punishing his insolence. Cannonballs hit all around him, some within a few feet, but he never flinched. His steadiness in the face of danger calmed the men down and enabled them to finish the redoubt and prepare for the attack of British infantry later in the day.

Many others could be named. Some, such as Nathan Hale, are a little more familiar to modern readers. Hale was a twenty-one year old teacher who volunteered to scout the enemy positions the day after the British occupied New York. He was captured in civilian clothes and sentenced to hanging as a spy. Waiting with a calm and composure that impressed his captors, Hale is remembered for his final words, "I only regret that I have but one life to lose for my country." He had volunteered for the mission because, in his words, "I wish to be useful and every kind of service, necessary to the public good, becomes honorable by being necessary."[7]

It is the blatant disregard for the danger to their own lives that makes men like Prescott, Hale, Warren and Putnam heroes. They put their own lives on the line for a cause that they believed in. And perhaps that is the best place to start in a definition of the phrase "right to life." It was not so much their willingness to die. They recognized that all men die at some point. It was rather the desire to make their lives count for something before they died. It was the drive to make each individual life have significance.

The Meaning of Life

In its simplest form, the right to life means the obvious – that we have a right to live. No government can arbitrarily decide who will live and who will not without violating that right. The Fifth Amendment of the United States Constitution declares that no one can be "deprived of life" without "due process of the law."

The Founding Fathers believed that each person owned his life in much the same way that he owned property. An individual has as much right to his own life as he does to the land and possessions that are his. Almost inevitably in the writings of early America, we find "life" and "liberty" joined together. There was a recognition that the full enjoyment of life required liberty.

The right to life begins with the recognition that human beings have an intrinsic worth. The biblical view shows that God considers each person to be unique from the beginning.

> *For You formed my inward parts;*
> *You covered me in my mother's womb.*
> *I will praise You, for I am fearfully and*
> *wonderfully made;*
> *Marvelous are Your works,*
> *And that my soul knows very well.*
> *My frame was not hidden from You,*
> *When I was made in secret,*
> *And skillfully wrought in the lowest parts of the*
> *earth.*
> *Your eyes saw my substance, being yet unformed.*
> *And in Your book they all were written,*
> *The days fashioned for me,*
> *When as yet there were none of them.*
> (Psalm 139:13-16)

God not only knew us before we were born, he had purpose in mind for us after we were born. No one is thrown into the earth randomly. Every individual is here by design.

For I know the thoughts that I think toward you, says the LORD, thoughts of peace and not of evil, to give you a future and a hope. (Jeremiah 29:11)

In the ministry of Jesus we find that everything He did and said while He walked this earth was focused on the restoration of the individual to his God-given purpose. When Jesus said that He came to give life, He was talking about much more than just keeping the body breathing.

I have come that they may have life, and that they may have it more abundantly. (John 10:10)

Abundant life implies a good deal more than just getting by. It means living life to its fullest measure. It is experiencing a sense of fulfillment and satisfaction or contentment in life, something that only happens when we live out the purpose for which we were created. That purpose is most often found in the deepest desires that we have. The person who spent his whole childhood dreaming about becoming a doctor and then became a farmer probably is not experiencing abundant life. Likewise the person whose deepest desire is to farm should probably not become a doctor. Abundant life is wrapped up in the fulfillment of purpose.

The Old Testament concept of holiness is tied to abundant life. The word "holy" in Hebrew is *qodesh* (קֶדֶשׁ). It usually is defined as "set apart," and it does have that idea, but it means quite a bit more than just set apart. We can see it explained in Leviticus where it is the overriding theme. God commands us to be holy as He is holy.

The statutes that describe holiness apply to things as much as they do to people. Ground can be holy (Exodus 3:5). Garments can be holy (Exodus 28:2). The altar can be holy (Exodus 30:10). What makes things holy is not their behavior, since those things just mentioned do not have behavior. Rather they are holy because they are used for the purpose that they were made for.

Qodesh has the idea of completeness or wholeness. We can get an idea of what this means by looking at the opposite. Leviticus lists many things that are not holy.

> Do not have sexual relations with an animal and defile yourself with it. A woman must not present herself to an animal to have sexual relations with it; that is a perversion. (Leviticus 18:23)

The word "perversion" in this verse is tevel (בֶּל). It would be better translated "confusion" or "mixture." It refers to things being mixed that do not belong together. It is an idea that comes up whenever holiness is described. It relates to animals, to crops and even to clothes.

> Do not mate different kinds of animals. Do not plant your field with two kinds of seed. Do not wear clothing woven of two kinds of material. (Leviticus 19:19)

The central idea of unholiness, then, is confusion, and the central idea of holiness is purity of purpose.[8] Something is holy when it is exactly what it is supposed to be. It is pure, not confused or polluted. God is holy precisely because He is not the least bit confused about who He is or what His purpose is. We become holy when we develop an understanding of our purpose and then pursue it.

This idea of holiness is inherent in understanding the right to life. Every person has not only the right to live, but more importantly, the right to live out the God-given destiny that is inherent in his life. One of the primary purposes, if not the primary purpose, of

Something is holy when it is exactly what it is supposed to be.

government is to protect that right to pursue fulfillment.

John Witherspoon was the third President of Princeton University. He was an instructor to several of the delegates of the Continental Congress and had a marked influence on their development. Nine of those delegates graduated from Princeton and six of them had Witherspoon's signature on their diplomas. Witherspoon considered the right to life to be the single most important natural right. And he expected government to protect it.

> *The rights of subjects in a social state may be all summed up in protection, that is to say those who have surrendered part of their natural rights expect the strength of the public arm to defend and improve what remains. It ought to be observed that the only reward that a state can be supposed to bestow upon good subjects in general is protection and defense.* (John Witherspoon)

The first "unalienable right," then, the right to life, is really the right to pursue your purpose. The government's job is not to bring it to you. You still have to pursue it yourself, but you have a right to do so and if you do not attain it, you have no one to blame but yourself. Likewise, you do not have the right to prevent anyone else from attaining his or her destiny. In fact, you have a responsibility to protect the other person's right to life.

Abortion and the Right to Life

It becomes a responsibility for every citizen to find his purpose. When he does so, he benefits himself and he benefits society. It is not something that he can be forced into, however. Each individual must make the choices for himself. Because he has a right to life, he has power over his own life. He can do anything with it that he wants. But ultimately, sitting and watching television for a lifetime will not get anyone to fulfillment. Life has to be chosen.

He has power over his own life. He can do anything with it that he wants.

Whether a person chooses to pursue his purpose or not, he still has a responsibility to protect the right of others to pursue their purpose. This understanding of life brings up another subject that we believe needs to be addressed by every citizen. A significant portion of the opposition to abortion rests on the natural and unalienable right to life for the unborn child. To kill a child before it is born is to deprive it of the opportunity to fulfill his or her purpose.

That happens in America more than 4,000 times every day, 1.6 million times a year.[9]

There are two aspects of this issue that we want to discuss. First, and most obvious, is the right to life of the unborn child. But there is also the affect of abortion on the mother. Both involve the right to life.

Proponents of abortion use the Declaration of Independence as proof that abortion is a right. Right to life means having power over one's own life and that implies power over one's body. As such, a woman should have the right to choose for herself whether or not she will endure the rigors of a pregnancy.

The other side of the argument claims that the child itself has the same right to life and that the mother's rights end when they infringe on the natural rights of another. In other words, the mother's right to choose what to do with her body ends when the choice affects the life of the unborn child.

The whole issue, then, really revolves around whether or not the unborn child is actually a human being. At what point does the fetus become a person and thereby entitled to the unalienable rights that all human beings have?

We believe that the answer is so self-evident that it is amazing that any discussion of it is even necessary. From a biblical perspective, the fact that God saw our "substance" before it was even formed (Psalm 139:16) indicates that the person precedes the physical body, that the person is put into a body. We believe that the child becomes a human being at conception.

But even without considering the biblical perspective, the intention of the Founding Fathers seems pretty clear. We mentioned in the last chapter the influence that William Blackstone had on the delegates to the Continental Congress. Blackstone's own words indicate that he considered the unborn to be human.

> *Life is the immediate gift of God, a right inherent by nature in every individual; and it begins in the contemplation of law as soon as an infant is able to stir in the mother's womb. An infant en ventre sa mere, or in the mother's womb, is supposed in law to be born for many purposes.*

The thinking of early Americans about when life began is demonstrated by the fact that as early as 1821, there was already a state law in Connecticut that dealt directly with abortion and over the next half-century thirty-six state and territorial legislatures passed laws limiting abortion. They considered human life to begin long before birth.

There is also the fact that a fetus begins to function in numerous ways at a very early period. By the time most women know that they are pregnant, specific functions are already working. The heartbeat begins between eighteen and twenty-five days after conception. Electrical brain waves have been recorded as early as forty days. By the seventh week, facial features, toes and fingers are obvious. A fetus that is removed from the womb as early as twenty weeks from conception, can survive.[10]

Dr. and Mrs. J.C. Willke, in *Why Can't We Love Them Both*, give very simple criteria for determining human life. They ask and answer three questions:

1. Is this being alive? The answer is yes, he has criteria of life, meaning that he can reproduce his own cells and develop into maturity.
2. Is this being human? Yes, it is different from any other organism and it has completely human characteristics, including forty-six human chromosomes. It can develop into a mature human.
3. Is this being complete? Yes, nothing else needs to be added to it after conception.[11]

The reactions of women (and men, too, for that matter) who see models or pictures of a seven-week-old fetus indicate that it is rare to find anyone who really believes that the fetus is not a human being. When confronted with the facts, it is hard to deny. A small percentage of people still do, claiming that the baby is nothing but a mass of inhuman tissue, but it is a very small minority.

If the fetus is actually a human being – and we believe absolutely that it is – then abortion is a violation of the basic unalienable right to life for that child.

Life After Abortion

There is another serious aspect of the abortion issue that needs to be considered. It has been almost completely ignored until very recently. That is the condition known as Post Abortion Syndrome. Women who suffer from this will experience guilt, anxiety, emotional numbness, regret, shame, lowered self-esteem, depression, nightmares and flashbacks, often accompanied by other problems such as alcohol and drug abuse or broken marriages and relationships. Frequently there is hostility or even a hatred toward men. Crying suddenly for no reason is common. Most of the women reporting these symptoms did not belong to a church at the time, so the regrets are not generally a part of a religious upbringing.[12] Usually the symptoms don't show up for several years, typically five to ten.

The magnitude of abortion is staggering. As many as 44 percent of American women will have an abortion at some time during their lifetime.[13] Studies show that the majority of those will not really want the abortion. One study, for example, reported that 53 percent felt "forced" into the abortion by other people, usually a husband or boyfriend. 65 percent felt "forced" by circumstances; 83 percent said that they would have completed the pregnancy if they had been encouraged by one or more people to do so.[14]

There is no conclusive information about how many women experience Post Abortion Syndrome but even the most pro-abortion studies admit that there are at least some. The lowest study puts it at about 6 percent of those who have aborted children. Most studies range between 12 and 25 percent with some going as high as 50 percent.

The exact numbers are difficult to pin down for several reasons. Most significantly, the women who suffer the symptoms of Post Abortion Syndrome often don't say anything. Typically, in short-term studies done within six months of the abortion, 10 to 20 percent of the women report significant psychological problems which they associate with the abortion. But about 50 percent of the women who originally agreed to participate in the study later refused. That number is an indication of the avoidance behavior that is typical of Post Abortion Syndrome. In one study of 260 women who had negative reactions, about three-fourths said that there was a period of time, on average a little more than five years, when they would deny having any negative feelings at all.

Regardless of which study you accept, the majority of women who went to an abortion clinic did not really want to be there and felt at least some negative emotions regarding the procedure. In one study of patients just eight weeks after an abortion, 54 percent complained of nervous

As many as 44 percent of American women will have an abortion at some time.

disorders, 36 percent had sleep disturbances and 31 percent already felt remorse over their decision. 25 percent had visited psychiatrists, compared to only 3 percent of the control group. Overall, it is probably safe to say that more than three-fourths of the women who have abortions pay for it with years or even a lifetime of remorse, depression, anguish and physical problems.

A host of medical conditions can be added to these psychological problems. Women who abort are twice as likely to become heavy smokers. They are twice as likely to develop breast cancer and more than twice as likely to develop cervical, ovarian or liver cancer.

All of this might make you wonder why anyone would have an abortion in the first place. It is significant that the "counseling" that is given at abortion clinics inevitably assures the women that the fetus is not a baby, that it is just a mass of tissue, that the procedure will not be painful and that there will be no negative side effects. None of these statements is true but they are made to bring some calm before the abortion is performed. Women are never told about the level of psychological and physical risk involved.

Once those concerns are eliminated, the decision to have an abortion can be made without any reference to the fetus. It is only the interests of the mother that are important. In the infamous *Roe vs. Wade* decision in 1973, the Supreme Court cited the mother's health as the primary justification for abortion. Health was defined mostly in terms of the mother's desire to avoid having to take on an unwanted responsibility. Supreme Court Justice Douglas referred to the mother having to:

> *endure the discomforts of pregnancy; to incur the pain, higher mortality rate, and aftereffects of childbirth; to abandon educational plans; to sustain loss of income; to forego the satisfactions of careers; to tax further mental and physical health in providing childcare, and in some cases to bear the lifelong stigma of unwed motherhood.*

As we have seen, the risks for Post Abortion Syndrome associated with having an abortion seem to drastically outweigh the benefits of "educational plans," "careers," and having to provide childcare. Post Abortion Syndrome has tremendous potential to destroy careers, relationships and health. There is a serious problem with the whole approach to abortion that is not explained to most women until it is too late.

The Essence of Motherhood

Susan Star Sered, in her book *Priestess, Mother, Sacred Sister*, examined a variety of religions that were female dominated, meaning that they were started by women and, in all but one, the entire membership was women. The theory was that a religious setting where the issues of life most important to the participants would manifest themselves without any male influence could provide an opportunity to determine what issues were truly most important to women, as opposed to what men thought was most important to women.

Sered's findings demonstrated that the core of how women defined their own "womanhood" was in "motherhood." In virtually every society that she studied, the role of a wife was considered subservient and weak whereas the role of a mother was looked upon as strong. The religious expression of those groups used terms and imagery taken from the process of childbirth and the raising of children. The final summary of her findings emphasizes the aspect of motherhood above all else.

> *What does receive attention and elaboration in these religions is women's social roles as nurturers and healers, women's rights and responsibilities as primary childcare providers, women's emotional experiences of pain at the illness and death of children, women's social ties with other mothers, matrifocality, and women's proclivity for discovering the sacred which is immanent in this everyday world of care and relationship.*[15]

Numerous gender studies confirm Sered's conclusions. One of the primary differences between men and women is the way in which they perceive themselves. Men think in terms of achievement, women in terms of relationships. We experience the greatest sense of failure in life when the foundation of our identity is threatened. For men, that core is in what they achieve. Men commit suicide at a rate seven to eight times higher than women in this culture. It is almost always connected to a sense of social humiliation because of a failure in business. For women, the crisis that leads to suicide is inevitably tied to the loss of a loved object, particularly the loss of a child.[16]

If we are right in saying that a woman's sense of identity is closely tied to motherhood – and there are many more studies than the couple that we have referenced here that say so – then the act of abortion is a self-inflicted wound that strikes at the very core of her sense of purpose in life. It is a kind of psychological suicide. It is no wonder that Post Abortion Syndrome is so prevalent.

Which brings us back to the point we made at the beginning of this chapter. We defined life, in both the biblical sense and in terms of the right to life intended by the Declaration of Independence, as the right to pursue your purpose. By allowing abortion to continue as a legally sanctioned alternative to responsible parenting, we are not only denying the unborn child the right to life, but we are curtailing the ability of women who have abortions to live out their own purpose. We are creating a deception that discloses from them the fact that they are depriving themselves of life as much as they are the child.

We are not saying that women must be relegated to simply having children in order to be godly. Scripture makes it clear that women have always had careers. A simple reading of Proverbs 31 shows how involved women can be in all kinds of business. But the effects of abortion keep women from experiencing the satisfaction, fulfillment and peace that every part of life is supposed to have. Instead, they are consigned to guilt, depression anxiety and the loss of relationship that are the natural biological results of abortion.

We do not want to leave the discussion of abortion on such a negative note, however. There is healing and there is hope for women who suffer from Post Abortion Syndrome. It inevitably involves confronting that fact that they have actually taken the life of another person through abortion and asking God for forgiveness. The experience of women who have found healing through God's grace tells us that one of the most important elements of that process is the presence of another person who does not judge them but rather loves them unconditionally. When any of us speak against abortion, we need to keep that part of the message in mind. The women who had an abortion without a full understanding of what they were doing have as much right to life as anyone else.

We have focused on abortion in this chapter, but the same principle holds true for anything that tends to restrict the enjoyment of a fulfilling life. Addictions will remove real life. Isolation will remove real life. Intolerance of others will remove real life. Recognizing the right to life has as much to do with learning to forgive others of their transgressions as it does in being forgiven of ours.

Choosing life means determining to choose those things that will lead to the fulfillment of your destiny. It means determining not to choose those things that will take away the enjoyment of life. When we do that, we will find that we are able to bring life to all of those around us.

---

[1]Fleming, *Now We Are Enemies*, pg. 123.

[2]Ketchum, *Decisive Day*, pg. 194-195.

[3]Fleming, *Now We Are Enemies*, pg. 58-59.

[4]*Ibid.*, pg. 245.

[5]*Ibid.*, pg. 157.

[6]*Ibid.*, pg. 159

[7]McDowell, *The Revolutionary War*, pg. 97.

[8]Wenham, *The New International Commentary on the Old Testament, The Book of Leviticus*, pg. 18-25.

[9]Elliot Institute website, David C. Reardon, Ph.D.

[10]www.abortionfacts.com, sponsored by Heritage House.

[11]*Ibid.*

[12]*Why Can't We Love Them Both.*

[13]Reisser and Reisser, *Healing After Abortion*, pg. 1.

[14]The statistics presented here are taken primarily from the Elliot Institute website.

[15]Sered, *Priestess, Mother, Sacred Sister*, pg. 286.

[16]Gaylin, *The Male Ego*, pg. 37.

★★★★★

Individual Right #7

The Right To Liberty

★★★★★

Responsibility #7

Be Personally Accountable

★★★★★

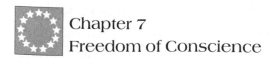

Chapter 7
Freedom of Conscience

Liberty of Conscience is every man's natural right, and he who is deprived of it is a slave in the midst of the greatest liberty. (William Penn)

Liberty was a ship, a merchant sloop owned by John Hancock, the man who would later become famous for his larger than life signature on the Declaration of Independence. It is perhaps fitting that the *Liberty* became the focal point for the first open conflict between the colonists and Great Britain over the question of liberty.

On June 10, 1768, British customs officials boarded the *Liberty* in Boston harbor and demanded to see the cargo. They suspected that Hancock was attempting to smuggle a cargo of Madeira wine into the country without paying the required import duties.

Hancock had all but begged for the British to suspect him. He had openly sworn not "to sell or to drink wine polluted by the payments of unconstitutional duties."[1] That didn't mean that he stopped drinking, though. Instead he became a smuggler.

The crew of the *Liberty*, rather than obeying the command from the customs officials, locked them in the ship's cabin and finished unloading the wine. Once the smuggled goods were safely ashore, the customs officials were unceremoniously thrown overboard.

A crowd of Boston citizens, upon hearing what was transpiring, gathered along the docks and became so unruly that they seized the Collector and the Controller and drove them through the streets. The Collector's son was dragged along by his hair. The other Commissioners of the Customs, hearing the commotion from their office, fled for their lives. They took refuge in Castle William in Boston Harbor until the riot settled down.

It did not take long, of course, for the British to respond to this affront to legal agents of the government. The Royal Navy intervened by seizing the *Liberty*. Crewmen from *HMS Halifax* towed the merchantman away from the dock.

The problem is that liberty means a lot of different things to different people.

Hancock never got his ship back. It was fitted out in April, 1769 to patrol off the coast of Rhode Island for smugglers. The following summer, the crew of the *Liberty*, while in Newport, abused Captain Joseph Packwood and created a violent reaction from the colonists who boarded the vessel and scuttled it. It was later burned.

What most Americans learn today is that the British tried to impose taxes without the consent of the colonists and that the colonists resisted and eventually rebelled against the government. The rallying cry of "no taxation without representation" became the slogan of freedom that we all associate with the second unalienable right, the "right to liberty." According to the traditional story, the Americans would have gladly paid the taxes if they had been represented in Parliament when the tax measures were passed. All that they asked was a say in their own affairs. All they asked was liberty.

The problem is that liberty means a lot of different things to different people. For John Hancock, the president of the Continental Congress at the time that the Declaration of Independence was signed, liberty meant the freedom to smuggle wine without paying taxes.

Taxation Without Representation

The beginning of all those taxes and the subsequent conflict is found in the conclusion of the French and Indian War. At least that was the name given to it in America. It was really a world-wide conflict primarily between Great Britain and France and it involved colonies of those two nations all around the globe. In Europe, it became known as the Seven Years War. The American part of the war was over by 1760 when the French lost all of their colonies in Canada. The war continued in Europe for another three years, until the Treaty of Paris in 1763.

The peace allowed Great Britain to shift its focus toward some developing problems in the American colonies. Ten thousand troops stationed there now had little to do. The Royal Navy, which had been scattered around the world through about twenty years of almost constant fighting, was now free to deal with other issues – such as colonial smuggling.

A series of tax measures were passed, beginning with the Molasses Act of 1733 and including names now infamous in American history – the Stamp Act, the Navigation Acts, the Townshend Act and the Tea Act, to name a few. The object of these taxes was to get the colonists to help reduce the immense debt that had accumulated during the French and Indian War. It was reasoned in Britain that the troops in America were there to defend the colonies against the French and the Indians so it was only reasonable that the colonies should help pay for them.

The colonists retorted that taxes passed by a Parliament in which not a single representative from the colonies was seated was an infringement on the rights of the citizens of English America.

A couple of things should be understood. First of all, colonial merchants experienced a great deal of affluence through the war and even afterward, until about 1770. They also did not pay very much in taxes compared to the average citizen in England.[2]

It was also not true that they were being completely excluded from representation in Parliament. Though the American writers and speakers used that argument to support their own position, especially James Otis and Benjamin Franklin, the fact is that influential leaders on both sides of the Atlantic were opposed to it.[3] Samuel Adams wrote against representation n 1765.

> *We are far however from desiring any Representation there, because we think the Colonies cannot be equally and fully represented; and if not equally then in Effect not at all.*

His cousin John Adams said much the same thing ten years later.

> *Would not representatives in the house of commons, unless they were numerous in*

proportion to the numbers of people in America,
be a snare rather than a blessing?

So "taxation without representation" made for good patriotic rhetoric but it was not exactly an accurate reflection of the desires of the colonists. Neither were the taxes really strangling the life out of them, at least not overtly. The rebellion of the American colonies was a very complicated issue that cannot be accurately understood in the simple terms that most Americans have learned their history. The whole economic structure of the British Empire played a part.

The Mercantile System

The concept of a colonial empire was that the colonies were a market for the goods and services of the mother country and in return they were aided by the investment of the mother country's capital which developed the resources of the colonies. With this in mind, Great Britain always placed a certain level of restriction on the trade of all British colonies. This basically meant that America agreed to trade with Britain and exclude everyone else in return for investment capital and a protected market. The arrangement has come to be known as the Mercantile System.

On the surface that sounds pretty simple. But there were problems that developed during the seventeenth century. Most of the investment capital from England went into the southern colonies. The primary export was tobacco, which was shipped through English warehouses to other markets around the world. A certain balance was kept up but generally the planters tended to be in debt to the British investors and therefore dependent on them. An imbalance existed where the colonies purchased much from England but didn't have enough being exported to keep up with the debts. As a result, there was a gradual loss of cash to pay off the balance. Cash went out but didn't come back.[4]

The only way that southern planters were able to keep up with the deficit was to expand their agricultural base by developing new lands to the west and to develop income through the fur trade. They did this by steadily encroaching on the Indian lands to the west.[5]

The same thing happened in New England, but on an even greater scale. Most of the things produced for export were the same things that English agriculture and industry produced. As a result there was not much demand in England for any of them, since the competition would have hurt the English. The exports that were encouraged were lumber, naval stores, furs, whale products and iron. At least the south had a product that England wanted. New England really didn't.[6]

New England purchased quite a bit from England, however, in the form of drygoods, hardware, notions and home furnishings. The result was a situation where New Englanders built up debt to the English merchants but were unable to bring money into the colonies to pay off the balance. There was very little capital investment in the northern colonies compared to the south, which made the situation even worse.[7]

In order to keep some balance to the trade, New England merchants engaged in a couple of technically illegal activities designed to bring money into the colonies so that they could pay the balances to Great Britain. During the 1600s, piracy became a huge portion of the New England economy. Privately owned ships were fitted out to prey on Spanish Caribbean fleets and even to roam as far as the Indian Ocean and the Red Sea.

After 1700 this source of revenue gradually disappeared as the European political situation changed and piracy became more dangerous.[8]

The other source of revenue came from smuggling. Merchants began to develop markets that bypassed the mother country and sold directly to other countries, such as Spain, France, Newfoundland and Nova Scotia. The biggest market was the sugar islands in the West Indies. By going directly to those markets, New England merchants avoided paying any taxes on any of the goods and they brought in much needed cash to make up for the money going to England to pay debts.[9]

Smuggling was largely ignored by British officials for the simple reason that it was so difficult to enforce. Through most of the early eighteenth century, Britain was at war with France or Spain or both and the resources that would have been needed to stop smuggling were tied up in other activities. It just wasn't worth it to enforce the law. As a result, the income from smuggling grew until it was an enormous part of the New England economy.

The Molasses Act of 1733, for example, made the West Indies trade illegal. Huge import duties were imposed on sugar, molasses and rum that did not come through regular, legal channels.[10] Nevertheless, by 1750, Rhode Island imported 11,500 hogsheads of molasses through illegal means compared to 2,500 from the British sources. In Massachusetts, the difference was 14,500 smuggled hogsheads to 500 legal. Smuggling became far more important than the legal trade.[11]

A couple of factors began to change the British apathy toward smugglers, however. The first actually did have a connection to representation in the Parliament. The sugar trade in the West Indies became so lucrative that plantation owners there dreamed of making a fortune, moving back to England and living the life of country gentlemen while their plantations were run by overseers. Many of them sought positions in Parliament in keeping with their genteel image of themselves. By 1770 there were over seventy seats held by men with economic interests in the West Indies. In any situation that involved choosing between the sugar trade and the American colonies, the colonists were guaranteed to lose.[12]

The life of leisure led most plantation owners to become somewhat lazy in their management and it wasn't long before the whole system was extremely inefficient. The soil became less productive and the competition became greater. France, Spain, Holland and Denmark developed sugar plantations of their own on the islands that they controlled and the general practice of those planters made their enterprises much more productive. The soil was not as worn out. They practiced diversification, alternating things like coffee with the sugar, thus replenishing the ground. They developed their markets to the level that they could undersell the British owners by as much as 25 to 40 percent.[13]

It was the New England merchants that made the British angry, however. They tended to trade directly with the foreign competition to the detriment of the British. It was especially infuriating when Britain was at war with those nations. The colonists didn't seem to care. Business was business.

Since the planters had seats in Parliament, they were able to get considerable legislation passed to try to force the economy into their favor. The problem was that the American colonists tended to ignore them.

With the Treaty of Paris in 1763, however, things began to change. The French were no longer a problem in Canada and the troops that had been along the border could now deal with the colonists. The ships of the Royal Navy could now be stationed to patrol various American shipping areas for smugglers. The British began to crack down heavily on the illegal business activities. The primary purpose of most of the tax measures that the colonists resisted was to deal with the colonial trade.

Writs of Assistance were issued to enable customs officials to search for contraband anywhere that they wanted to. Naval vessels were given authorization to search American ships anywhere that they found them. Customs officials were stationed in every major city in America. A vice-admiralty court was set up in 1764 to deal with American cases. Spying was encouraged by offering to share sequestered cargoes with informers.[14] With smuggling curtailed, New England merchants were hard-pressed to make ends meet.

With smuggling curtailed, New England merchants were hard-pressed to make ends meet.

The southerners had similar problems. The Proclamation Line of 1763 closed all of the western land to settlement by the southern land speculators. At the same time it made the fur trade illegal for the same colonists.[15] A case can be made for the idea that the colonists were not as much concerned about philosophical rights as they were by the fact that British restrictions were beginning to work and it was putting the Americans into a position where their survival would depend on complete subservience to the British crown. That did not sit well with them.

The Stubborn American

In spite of the evidence to the contrary, however, the rhetoric from the period indicates that philosophical principles did play a significant part in American resistance to Great Britain. A tremendous amount of effort was devoted to justifying the rebellion in the eyes of the world. That was the purpose for the Declaration of Independence. "A decent respect to the opinions of mankind requires that they should declare the causes which impel them to the separation." The causes were then stated as the unalienable rights of man.

The issue over taxation illustrated a fundamental difference in thinking between Americans and Englishmen. The Americans were very independent. Over the two centuries since the first settlements, they had learned to be completely self-sufficient. The British were too far away to be of much help. A request sent to the king or to Parliament could require as much as a year to get a response. The colonists had no choice but to learn to fend for themselves.

Most of them came to America precisely because they wanted to get away from the immediate control of the government in the first place. That was true of the Pilgrims. It was true of the Quakers who settled in Pennsylvania. It was true of the settlers in the backwoods. Self-sufficiency was the one characteristic that best described the average American colonist. It was a matter of survival.

As time went on, that trait became a natural part of American life. In every culture in the world you can find those who simply don't like to be told what to do. But only in America has it been turned into a lifestyle. Most Americans idolize the rebel, the independent soul who defies authority. It is Americans who can be manipulated into doing something by simply daring them. We tend to do some things for no other reason than because someone told us not to.

To a large extent, that seems to have been the temperament of the early Americans. One gets the impression that they would have defied the British for no other reason than because soldiers appeared to make them obey. It almost seems as though they would have rebelled even if it meant destroying their own income rather than protecting it. The English, and for that matter, most Europeans, had some difficulty understanding the American way of thinking. This stubborn independence was unique to Americans. Liberty truly was more important to them than anything else in life.

The bad side of this was the stubbornness that resulted from it. The good side was that it made Americans more likely to be completely responsible for themselves. The concept of a welfare state is fairly recent in America. In the early years, if you didn't work, you didn't eat. Americans have always been very generous but they have also been proud. We like to think that we can take care of ourselves without help from anyone – and most of the time we can.

The second unalienable right of the Declaration of Independence is the right to liberty. Liberty brings the freedom to make choices. Choice brings accountability. If we make a choice, then we can no longer blame anyone else. The right to liberty carries with it accountability.

Life Isn't Fair

Life is not fair. It never has been. In fact, "fair" is really a four-letter word. The desire for life to be fair makes you spend your time looking at other people. Instead of enjoying what you do have, you keep looking at what you don't have. As long as "fair" is in your vocabulary, you will have envy, jealousy, greed, lust, selfish ambition and anger. As long as fair is in your vocabulary, you will never be able to experience the liberty that is your unalienable right.

We each are dealt a different set of circumstances. Liberty means that we have the freedom to make choices that can improve life. Nothing guarantees that you will make the right choices and, if you don't, no one is responsible but you.

"Fair" is usually thought of in negative terms. When people think that they have lost out on something, they claim it isn't fair.

But fairness has a positive side, too. It isn't fair that America is so blessed. The poorest person in America is better off than most of the world. According to Heritage Foundation political scientist Robert Rector, when the official measure of poverty in the United States was developed in 1963, a "poor" American family had twenty-nine times greater per capita income than the average for the rest of the world.[16]

It just isn't fair that we should have so much. But so many still think that the world or the government owes them something. The unalienable right to liberty does not mean that life will be fair.

Neither does the Bible promise that life is fair. God gave His chosen people things that they didn't do anything to deserve. They occupied cities that they did not build and houses full of good things that they did not fill. They took over wells that they did not dig and vineyards and olive trees that they did not plant (Deuteronomy 6:10-11). It wasn't fair.

But they then had to become accountable for what they did with the things that they had. When they made wrong choices they lost what they had. And it was not the fault of anyone else.   Babylon and Assyria became instruments of judgment but it was not the Babylonians and the Assyrians who were the real problem.   It was the failure of God's people to make responsible and personally accountable choices.

> *I brought you into a bountiful country,*
> *To eat its fruit and its goodness.*
> *But when you entered, you defiled My land*
> *And made My heritage an abomination.*
> (Jeremiah 2:7)

Liberty is not a matter of everyone being given the same thing. If we divided the wealth of America equally between every citizen, it would be a very short time before those that have it now would have it back again. They are the ones who do the most with what they have. They don't assume that anyone owes them anything. They take responsibility for their lives and stop blaming others for their misfortunes.

The Parable of the Talents reflects just what God thinks of fairness.

> *For the kingdom of heaven is like a man*
> *traveling to a far country, who called his own*
> *servants and delivered his goods to them. And to*
> *one he gave five talents, to another two, and to*
> *another one, to each according to his own ability.*
> (Matthew 25:14-15)

The amount given to each one depended on his ability, not on what was fair. When the man came back to see what they had done with the talents, his judgment of them was not based on how much he had given them. It was a matter of what they did with what they had. The servant who did nothing with it was called "wicked and lazy" (Matthew 25:26).

It is interesting to compare Israel before the reign of King Saul and Israel after they had a king. Before that time, we are told that there was not much order.

> *In those days there was no king in Israel; everyone did what was right in his own eyes.* (Judges 21:25)

We are accustomed to thinking of that verse as describing a great evil where there was no restraint on the people. In a sense that was true. But consider how God reacted when the people asked for a king.

> *And the LORD said to Samuel, "Heed the voice of the people in all that they say to you; for they have not rejected you, but they have rejected Me, that I should not reign over them.* (1 Samuel 8:7)

The one thing that was missing was personal accountability. The people of Israel wanted a king who would bring accountability without them having do be personally responsible.

Liberty is not about being fair. It is about having the opportunity to make choices and then being accountable for them. Freedom necessarily implies accountability. You cannot blame others for your failures. Neither do you have any inherent right to the property of others just because they have more than you.

The Meaning of Liberty

When the Founders of America spoke of Liberty, they weren't always in agreement about just what that meant. They had to find common ground in their thinking before they could establish the United States as a land of freedom.

When the delegates to the Constitutional Convention arrived in Philadelphia in 1787, they faced an almost impossible task. They had to forge a workable government that would cut across regional and cultural differences that were nearly insurmountable. It is nothing short of a miracle that they were even able to agree on a meeting, much less the finished Constitution.

The cultures of north and south, east and west were so different that they might as well have been different countries.

The cultures of north and south, east and west were so different that they might as well have been different countries. John Adams wrote in 1775 from the Continental Congress, "the characters of gentlemen in the four New England colonies differ from those in the others . . . as much as several distinct nations almost." He was most concerned that the differences could not be overcome. "Without the utmost caution on both sides and the most considerate forbearance with one another and prudent condescension on both sides, they will certainly be fatal."[17] After the war, Washington commented on the same problem. "Thirteen sovereignties, pulling against each other, and all tugging at the federal head, will soon bring ruin on the whole."[18]

Liberty was such an integral part of the deliberations at both the Continental Congress and the Constitutional

Convention that we should look at what they did mean. It has all become a part of our heritage.

David Hackett Fischer, in *Albion's Seed*, his study of the British folkways that were transferred to early America, identifies four principle divisions of culture in early America – the Puritan culture of New England, the royalist culture of Virginia, the Quakers of Pennsylvania and the backcountry culture of the frontier. Each group migrated from a different part of England and so had distinctive characteristics that set it apart from the others. Our concern here is with the concepts of liberty within each region.

The Puritans of New England

The Puritans began with a heavily religious foundation. Their concept of liberty was very much colored by those beliefs. There were four ways that they conceived of liberty.[19]

The first was the liberty of the community, "publick liberty" in the phrase common at the time. It involved close restraints on individuals, something not unusual in a religious community. But for Puritans, it meant that they had the liberty to impose those restraints on themselves. They reacted violently when outsiders tried to impose restraints on them. Liberty meant the freedom of the community to impose its own regulations.[20]

The second form of liberty for a Puritan is backwards to modern thinking. Puritans conceived of themselves as living under certain restraints imposed on them. Today we think of people as starting from freedom and having restraints imposed. To the Puritan it was the other way around. They started with restraints and were given exemption from them. This largely concerned the written laws. For example, a law could be enacted which extended "liberties and privileges of fishing and fowling" to certain individuals, but denied those liberties to others. This might be called "individual liberty." It showed a concern with relating to the community as a whole.[21]

A third type of liberty in the Puritan mind was what they called "soul liberty." It was by far the most important in their thinking. Soul liberty basically meant the freedom to serve God in this world. It was a kind of obligation to God. They did not think in terms of religious freedom as

★★★★★

All four of these freedoms in the Puritan mind were a sense of ordered liberty.

★★★★★

we now think of it or even of religious tolerance. Rather it was a freedom to worship God within the context of Puritan belief. Such liberty was not considered to be a contradiction with persecution of Quakers, Catholics, Baptists, Presbyterians or Anglicans. If you did not worship within the narrow framework of true faith as they understood it, then you did not have the freedom to worship at all.[22]

A fourth liberty was the freedom from the tyranny of circumstance. The Massachusetts poor laws were designed to insure that no one starved.[23] This does not mean that anyone was free from the responsibility to work. Work ethic was a significant part of Puritanism, but when circumstances left a person destitute, the community stepped in to meet the need.

All four of these freedoms in the Puritan mind were a sense of ordered liberty. Not all of these ideas came into the Declaration of Independence completely unaltered but even today there are traces of them in our beliefs.

The Anglicans of Virginia

When Sir William Berkeley became governor of Virginia in 1641, he recruited heavily for immigrants among the Royalist elite of southern and western England, the cavaliers, as they were known. His efforts were aided by the success of the Puritans during the English Civil War and the subsequent persecution of the Anglican Royalists.

They brought with them the attitudes of the English nobility and the religious beliefs of the Anglican Church, with all of its formality and ritual. Their views of liberty were more elitist than the New Englanders ever dreamed of.

To put it simply, Virginians believed that liberty was the power to rule over others without being ruled over by others.[24] Freedom meant dominion and the more one ruled, the more freedom one had. The opposite of ruling was slavery.

The dominion extended to dominion over oneself, a very important aspect of liberty. As John Randolph said, "Life is not so important as the duties of life."[25] In other words, the Royalist thinking did not allow for license as a part of liberty. The more liberty a person had, the greater responsibility he had to be accountable to his duty to society.

Virginians considered liberty to be a birthright. It never occurred to them in the early years that liberty belonged to everyone.[26] Thomas Jefferson, in comparing New Englanders to Virginians in a letter to a friend, described those in the north as "jealous of their liberties and those of others," while those in the south were "zealous for their own liberties but trampling on those of others."[27] He was from the south himself. This attitude evolved but it did not really disappear until after the Civil War, and even then it could still be found to some degree.

This view of liberty made the southern colonies very sensitive to any attempt by the government of England to control them. Individual independence was prized even more than in New England.

Of course, there were some obvious contradictions in the system. They thought nothing of enslaving others. Dr. Samuel Johnson once noted this paradox. "How is it," he asked, "that we hear the loudest yelps for liberty among the drivers of negroes?"[28] Slavery played a significant part in the southern economy until the Civil War, and even then it was not given up willingly. But there is a sense in which this attitude contributed to the later resistance to Great Britain. Edmund Burke, speaking in Parliament, understood the underlying force of liberty in Virginia, in spite of slavery.

> . . . *a circumstance attending these colonies . . . makes the spirit of liberty still more high and haughty than in those to the northward. It is, that in Virginia and the Carolinas, they have a vast multitude of slaves. Where this is the case in any part of the world, those who are free are by far the most proud and jealous of their freedom.*
>
> *Freedom is to them not only an enjoyment, but a kind of rank and privilege. Not seeing there that freedom, as in countries where it is a common blessing and as broad and general as the air, may be united with much abject toil, with great misery, with all the exterior of servitude, liberty looks amongst them like something that is more noble and liberal.*

> *I do not mean, Sir, to commend the superior morality of this sentiment, which has at least as much pride as virtue in it; but I cannot alter the nature of man. The fact is so; and these people of the southern colonies are much more strongly, and with a higher and more stubborn spirit, attached to liberty than those to the northward. . . . In such a people, the haughtiness of domination combines with the spirit of freedom, fortifies, it, and renders it invincible.*[29]

In other words, seeing the bondage of slavery first hand, the southerners became even more appreciative of and passionate about the freedom that they had.

The contradictions became obvious in time to men like Jefferson and Washington, who wrote against slavery, even though they owned slaves, and eventually made provisions to free their slaves. The individual passion for liberty drove them to resist control and develop the arguments against tyranny over themselves and the colonies. The sense of responsibility to duty that was a part of the Royalist conception of liberty eventually made it clear to them that liberty belonged to all men, even the slaves.

The Backcountry

The early 1700s saw a migration of people from northern Ireland and the border areas between England and Scotland that populated the backcountry of America, those areas west of Virginia and Pennsylvania. They were people who were accustomed to the relatively lawless areas of Great Britain where family feuds and violent justice had been common through most of their history. By settling in very remote areas of the New World, the fierce independence was magnified and developed into a perception of liberty that was vastly different from any other part of America.

To the people of the backcountry, liberty generally meant not having to answer to any government at all. The sparse population made any kind of centralized government almost impossible and the independent nature of the people made them likely to reject much government anyway.[30]

This does not mean that anarchy reigned, however. There were certain community standards of behavior that were recognized and deviation from those standards was not tolerated. But difference of opinion was not tolerated either.

The best example of this culture among the Founding Fathers was Patrick Henry. He made a reputation for himself as a lawyer during a case that became known as "The Parsons' Cause." In his presentation, he declared that the king of England, by nullifying a law that had been passed by the local Virginia government, had forfeited his right to obedience by the colonists.[31] In other words, no one, not even the king of the Parliament, was going to dictate law to him.

This fierce independence is an undercurrent to most of the thinking of modern Americans on how liberty should be defined. It is a liberty that is focused intensely on individual rights and responsibilities.

The Quakers of Pennsylvania

The closest thing to our modern conception of liberty was the beliefs of the Friends in Pennsylvania, known commonly as the Quakers. These refugees from religious persecution in England were more sensitive than most to restrictions to religious freedom.

William Penn, the founder of the colony, called it "liberty of conscience."[32] Where the Puritans believed everyone had the liberty to do what was right, or more accurately, what was right in the Puritan interpretation of things, the Quakers were convinced that everyone even had a right to believe what was wrong.[33]

Penn was the primary spokesman of this view. The quote at the beginning of this chapter is one example of the multitude of statements he made in defense of individual liberty. There are many others, such as this one.

No man is so accountable to his fellow creatures as to be imposed upon, restrained or persecuted for any matter of conscience whatever.

Most Quakers had experienced severe persecution in England because of their religious beliefs. They were determined not to let it happen in the New World. Until long after the Revolutionary War, Pennsylvania was the only colony that practiced genuine religious toleration.

Liberty of conscience extended to other fundamental rights to a greater degree than in the other colonies. The right to ownership of property and trial by jury were especially prominent.

Pennsylvania became the one colony in which all rights claimed by the ruling group, namely the Quakers, were extended to everyone else. Pennsylvania was the first colony to persistently pursue the complete abolition of slavery. They did it on purely moral grounds. Benjamin Franklin, though not a

Quaker himself (he was a Presbyterian), was actively involved in the anti-slavery movement through most of his life. Pennsylvania was the uncontested leader in abolition efforts.

The Quaker concept of liberty has had a lasting impression on the thinking of Americans. It produced a people who were fully committed to both the individual and to the community. Penn expressed the personal responsibility of the citizen in his *Frame of Government*:

> *Liberty without obedience is confusion, and obedience without liberty is slavery.*

It is not generally known by most Americans, but the Liberty Bell was originally forged to celebrate the fifty year anniversary of the founding of Pennsylvania. It is a fitting tribute to William Penn's ideals that it was inscribed with a quotation from Leviticus 25:10.

> *Proclaim Liberty throughout all the Land unto all the inhabitants thereof.*

In Pennsylvania, liberty truly was for all the inhabitants of the land.

Liberty Today

The task of forming a workable government out of these very different perceptions of liberty was perhaps the most difficult and yet the most significant part of the Constitutional Convention. Elements of all of them became fused into the American mentality, giving a view of liberty that is still with us today.

From the Puritans we have retained a couple of perceptions. We still think of liberty as the freedom to worship in any way that we see fit. As much as there is an attempt by a relatively small but vocal part of the population to stifle all public declarations of religious belief, the vast majority of Americans still think of themselves as Christians. We still believe that freedom to worship is vital to our liberty. Like the Puritans, we still believe that every individual should be free from the tyranny of circumstances and we are always anxious and willing to help those in need. Like the Virginians, we still believe that the greater our liberty, the more accountable we are to society. Like those in the backcountry, we still hate to have anyone tell us what to do, not even the government. We have retained a fanatical love of individualism and non-conformity. Like the Quakers, we still believe in the freedom of conscience.

What rings true in all of these concepts is the idea of individual freedom and individual responsibility. Every American has the right to believe whatever he wants to believe and to be whatever he chooses to be. But he also has a responsibility to his community, his country and to the rights of others. Accountability is inseparable from freedom.

---

[1] Quoted in Miller, *Origins of the American Revolution*, pg. 288.
[2] Wahlke, *The Causes of the American Revolution*, pg. 34-35.
[3] *Ibid.*, pg. 60.
[4] *Ibid.*, pg. 1.
[5] *Ibid.*, pg. 13.
[6] *Ibid.*, pg. 1.
[7] *Ibid.*, pg. 2.
[8] *Ibid.*, pg. 3.
[9] *Ibid.*
[10] *Ibid.*, pg. 5-6.

[11] *Ibid.*, pg. 6.

[12] *Ibid.*, pg. 5.

[13] *Ibid.*, pg. 5-6.

[14] *Ibid.*, pg. 11.

[15] *Ibid.*, pg. 14.

[16] Quoted by P.J. O'Rourke in *Parliament of Whores*.

[17] Bowen, *Miracle at Philadelphia*, pg. 91-92.

[18] *Ibid.*, pg. 33.

[19] Fischer, *Albion's Seed*, pg. 199.

[20] *Ibid.*, pg. 200-201.

[21] *Ibid.*, pg. 201-202.

[22] *Ibid.*, pg. 202-203.

[23] *Ibid.*, pg. 203-205.

[24] *Ibid.*, pg. 411.

[25] *Ibid.*, pg. 416.

[26] *Ibid.*, pg. 412.

[27] Bowen, *Miracle at Philadelphia*, pg. 92.

[28] Fischer, *Albion's Seed*, pg. 410.

[29] *Ibid.*, pg. 414.

[30] *Ibid.*, pg. 777-778.

[31] *Ibid.*, pg. 778.

[32] *Ibid.*, pg. 597.

[33] *Ibid.*

★★★★★

Individual Right #8

The Right To Own Property

★★★★★

Responsibility #8

Work

★★★★★

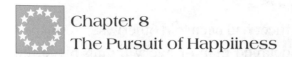

Chapter 8
The Pursuit of Happiiness

The Constitution only gives people the right to pursue happiness. You have to catch it yourself.
(Benjamin Franklin)

The first shot of the Revolutionary War was fired at the small Massachusetts village of Lexington on April 19, 1775. It was a rather confused affair. The British were on their way to Concord from Boston to look for weapons and ammunition that they believed the colonists were storing there. A handful of colonial militia, about seventy total, lined up across the village green with orders not to resist the 700 redcoats but to let them pass.[1]

No one really knows who fired first. Captain John Parker, concerned for his men, ordered them to disperse. Some did. Others did not. A shot rang out and the British responded. In seconds, eight colonists lay dead and nine wounded.[2] The troops continued on to Concord. There they began searching through the town for contraband supplies.

As the British searched from house to house, they showed a concern for private property that is not usually recognized by Americans today. A colonist named Timothy Wheeler had a storehouse full of flour that was intended for use by the militia in their resistance to the British. When a British officer demanded entrance, Wheeler let him in without argument. He put his hand on one of the barrels and declared,

"This is my flour. I am a miller, Sir. Yonder stands my mill. I get my living by it . . . this . . . is my flour; this is my wheat; this is my rye; this is mine."[3]

The British officer had been told otherwise. A spy had given the British a detailed map of every hiding place the colonists were using. But instead of pushing the issue, he merely declared, "Well, we do not injure private property."[4]

Numerous incidents were recorded in which British soldiers on that march asked for food or drink from the homes along the way, but insisted on paying for it. On one occasion, the British commander of the advance companies, Major Pitcairn, forced his way into a tavern owned by Ephraim Jones. Jones had three cannon hidden next door. Pitcairn angrily confiscated the cannon, returned to the tavern, had breakfast and then scrupulously paid for it.[5]

The British soldiers were Englishmen, after all, and despite the conflict about to erupt into open war, they had the same belief in the right to ownership of property that the colonists did. It was grounded in English history as far back as the Magna Carta. Voltaire wrote, "Liberty and property is the great national cry of the English."[6] In the bitterness of war there were exceptions on both sides but most of the time, at least at that early stage of the war, the British were careful to avoid violating the right to property.

We have lost some of the appreciation of this third unalienable right simply because it is not mentioned by that name in the Declaration of Independence. A couple of years earlier, the Continental Congress, in its first "Declarations and Resolves," used the phrase "life, liberty, and property."[7] In the Declaration, Jefferson changed it to the "pursuit of happiness."

This rather ambiguous phrase is a little misleading to modern readers. It has led many to assume that "happiness" is the end that they should seek in life. In fact, many have come to believe that America somehow owes them "happiness." A significant part of the appeal of presidential candidates is that they promise you that if you vote for them, they will make you happy. Your taxes will be less. Your work week will be shorter. You'll have more money for doing less work and you can spend your time lounging at home or

It has led many to assume that "happiness" is the end that they should seek in life.

going on vacations and you will be "happy." If you are unable to get a job, or perhaps just too lazy to get a job, then the government will give you money and that way you can be "happy" right along with everyone else. Most of us seem to believe that "happiness" is our right. For most people, happiness is associated with the enjoyment of pleasurable activities. It means contentment, fun, activities that make them smile or laugh. Even the biblical words for happy, *makarios* (μακάριος) in the New Testament and *'esher* (אֶשֶׁר) in the Old Testament, have the idea of being supremely blessed. Usually when people think of being happy, they mean little more than feeling good.

This belief means that the pursuit of happiness comes down to trying to order your life so that you can spend all your time feeling good. Most people work forty hours for no other reason than to get to the weekend so they can relax and feel good. They can hardly wait for five o'clock to roll around every day so they can get home, have dinner and plop themselves in front of the television where they can relax and feel good. They seek early retirement so that they can relax and feel good. How many times have you seen bumper stickers that say something like, "A bad day fishing is better than a good day working?" Work is almost never associated with "happy."

Everyone wants to be happy and life generally devolves into the pursuit of relaxation. Ultimately, they hope that they will go to heaven where they will sit on a cloud somewhere for eternity, feeling good and being happy.

Happiness in Work

Of all the myths of the American dream, this may be the most damaging. It was never quite the intent of the Founding Fathers, of course. No one owed "happiness" to anyone. As Franklin said, you have to "catch it yourself." We need to look very carefully at the concept of pursuing happiness.

Understand that we do not have any problem with being happy. Happiness is a good thing. But we do not believe that happiness is just feeling good or that it should be the primary goal of life. Human beings were not really created to just sit around and feel good. They were created to work. They were created to achieve. They were created to fulfill purpose and to accomplish and they can never really be happy in the truest sense of the word without it. Napoleon was once asked what he thought happiness was. He answered, "Happiness? The highest possible development of my talents."[8]

Work was not the result of sin. It was there before sin came into the world. Adam was put in the Garden of Eden to work.

> *Then the* LORD *God took the man and put him
> in the garden of Eden to tend and keep it.* (Genesis
> 2:15)

If work was not a result of sin, then what changed when sin entered the world? The answer is the meaningfulness of the work. Prior to the fall, Adam worked in the garden, but his work was tied to his purpose. Afterwards, he had to do work that was often nothing more than survival. Suddenly there were weeds to pull and obstacles to his work that had not been there before. Suddenly work became drudgery. Sin didn't bring work. Rather it robbed work of its purpose.

We all know people who love the work they do. There may not be many of them around, but there are some. They never seem to get tired. They can work long hours and it doesn't seem to bother them. They love what they do. They are people who have found purpose in their work. For them, happiness is directly tied to their work.

You may not think that you could ever find purpose in your work. The truth is that the greatest purpose is to provide security and stability for your family. If that is the only purpose you find, work will still become more bearable, even if it is a job you don't particularly like.

We were always intended to work. It was never optional. Those who learn to work enjoy life more than those who just want to play all the time. When they look back on life they feel a greater level of satisfaction and a greater sense of accomplishment.

It is with this fact in mind that we can understand the pursuit of happiness. The Founding Fathers certainly believed in the value of a good work ethic. In fact, the first coin authorized by the new government of the United States, in 1787, did not have the phrase on it that we are so familiar with today – "In God We Trust." That was not added to any American money until 1865. Rather, the first coin had the motto "Mind Your Business." It was modeled after a design by Benjamin Franklin and was intended to connect the currency of the country with the idea that business and work ethic were a significant part of the foundation of a strong nation.

The greatest goal in life for most people in early America was to own their own land.

It was this concept that the Founders had in mind when they wrote "pursuit of happiness" into the Declaration. As with most of the thinking of Thomas Jefferson and the other Founders, the concepts that became the Declaration of Independence were not original with them. They came from other philosophers and thinkers of an earlier time. As we said earlier, John Locke was one of the most significant. The phrase "life, liberty and the pursuit of happiness" probably came from Vattel, but the concept behind it was directly from Locke's writing.

Locke didn't use the word "happiness," however. He called it the "pursuit of property." By that, he implied a great deal more than simply the ownership of material goods and land.

In our modern society, where the majority of the population lives in large cities, working in offices and factories, it is difficult to grasp the importance that people of the seventeenth century placed on property. In an agricultural society, everything depends on the land. The greatest goal in life for most people in early America was to own their own land. When they did, they had achieved stability for their families and provided their children with a heritage. Property gave security.

The Founding Fathers associated property with hard work and success. They frequently referred to the baser sort of person as the one who had no character and no property. In a land that was three fourths agricultural, where anyone who wanted to work could acquire land, there was no excuse not to. If you did not have property, it was almost certainly because you were lazy.[9]

In the minds of those living in Locke's age, property was not just stuff that you owned. It was the fruit of your labor. It was the visible, tangible evidence of a person's life goals being fulfilled.

This is certainly the biblical concept. Throughout Scripture, the possession of land and goods indicates stability for the family. If someone in ancient Israel had to sell his land, he had the right to buy it back. In fact, even if he did not buy it back, it returned to him during the Year of Jubilee.

> *But if he is not able to have it restored to himself, then what was sold shall remain in the hand of him who bought it until the Year of Jubilee, and in the Jubilee it shall be released, and he shall return to his possession.* (Leviticus 25:28)

Land was to always be returned to the family. God called the failure to recognize these property rights oppression.

Therefore you shall not oppress one another,
but you shall fear your God; for I am the LORD
your God. (Leviticus 25:17)

When Jefferson wrote "the pursuit of happiness," he was referring directly to the concept that John Locke called "the pursuit of property." In the thinking of the Founding Fathers, happiness was not sitting around being comfortable and not having to work. It was not having the ability to take every weekend and spend it at the lake. It was not three weeks of vacation every year. Happiness was seeing the fruit of your labor result in property that would provide security for your family. Happiness was the result of successful labor. The property that resulted from labor could not legally be taken away from anyone.

Each individual of the society has a right to
be protected by it in the enjoyment of his life,
liberty, and property, according to standing laws.
He is obliged, consequently, to contribute his
share to the expense of this protection, and to give
his personal service or an equivalent, when
necessary. But no part of the property of any
individual can, with justice, be taken from him, or
applied to public uses, without his own consent,
or that of the representative body of the people.
In fine, the people of this commonwealth are not
controllable by any other laws than those to which
their constitutional representative body have
given their consent. (John Adams)

The Pursuit of Property

Property was very important to the Founding Fathers but it must never be forgotten that they associated property with successful work. This was the main reason that voting, in the years before the Revolution, was restricted to landowners.[10] It was felt that the fact a man owned property indicated that he had a good work ethic and that he was therefore qualified to handle the responsibility of choosing those who would govern. In a country with wide-open frontiers, anyone who did not have land was likely to be indigent and, if he didn't care enough about the land to commit his life to it, he didn't have the necessary qualifications to vote wisely. This concept is what he had in mind when Jefferson wrote about the right to own property in a free country.

The true foundation of republican government is the equal right of every citizen, in his person and in his property . . . In the American states, every one may have land to labor for himself, if he chooses.[11]

He then declared that the effort of investing time and work in that property caused a person to have a vested interest in the affairs of the country.

Every one, by his property or by his satisfactory situation, is interested in the support of law and order.[12]

Jefferson's meaning was that those who did not have property could not be trusted to make the best decisions.

Such men may safely and advantageously reserve to themselves a wholesome control over their public affairs, and a degree of freedom which in the hands of the canaille (the lowest class of people) *of the cities of Europe, would be instantly perverted to the demolition and destruction of everything public and private.*[13]

When the Constitutional Convention decided not to require the ownership of land as a requirement for the right to vote, they radically departed from a very old standard. They felt that every person living in the country had personal rights, which included the idea of a government only by the consent of the governed. Suffrage was extended to all men. But the concepts of work ethic did not go away. Everyone still believed that those who worked were the most qualified to run the community and the nation and those who did not were unworthy of either charity or sympathy. They would have cringed at the welfare programs in place today.

Socialism in Early America

In 1606, King James I of England signed a charter that created two new companies, the Plymouth Company and the London Company, which later became known as the Virginia Company. His goal was to solidify British claims to North America by establishing viable colonies there.

The Plymouth Company was short-lived and had no real impact on the history of America. It planted a colony at the mouth of the Kennebec River in what is now Maine, but within a couple of years, the settlers had all returned to England.

The London Company, on the other hand, proceeded to establish the first permanent colony in America, what we know today as Jamestown. Three ships set out in December of 1606, the *Susan Constant*, the *Godspeed* and the *Discovery*. Aboard were 140 colonists, recruited through an intense advertising campaign that promised great riches and land in the New World.

Adverse winds delayed sailing by six weeks, depleting food supplies. By the time they reached Virginia, forty-five had died. The rest straggled ashore at the mouth of the Powhatan River, which they renamed the James, in honor of the king. They built a fort and established themselves in their new home, Jamestown.

The suffering that they underwent over the next few years almost defies description. The heat of the summer was debilitating. The location that they chose was near a low-lying wetlands area that spawned swarms of insects. They suffered from typhus, starvation, foul water, Indian attacks and harsh winters. More colonists kept coming, which made the supply situation even worse. Hundreds died over the first few years.

For our study, there are a couple of things that we should note about Jamestown. First of all, a preponderance of the colonists were gentleman adventurers. They were pseudo aristocrats and lesser nobility who considered themselves to be gentlemen and who, for the most part, had not done a day of actual labor in their entire lives. They had decided to come to America because they found themselves out of place in an overpopulated London that could not support them. For the most part, they really believed that they could make their fortunes in the New World and live in the lifestyle of comfort and leisure to which they felt entitled. They tended to be very unwilling to cooperate with each other or with the local natives and they felt betrayed when the colony did not provide them with easy riches. They expected to find gold just lying around. In fact, one of them set sail back to England loaded down with a treasure that turned out to be nothing more than fool's gold and dirt. But the atmosphere was more like the gold rush days in California than one of serious settlers who intended to plant their roots and stay. There was not much incentive in the Jamestown colony to actually work.

A second problem was in the Virginia Charter itself. The agreement was that all members of the expedition would hold all property in common. As they worked, the goods that they produced would be shared equally by the entire colony. As a result, it wasn't long before people stopped working very hard. There was no reason to. They could always live off of the hard work of others. The outcome of such tendencies was a disaster for the colony. In spite of the abundance of resources around them, the Jamestown colony nearly starved to death.

Disease struck and with the increasing problems, dissension manifested itself. Councilor George Kendall was accused of sowing discord and was arrested, tried and shot. The first president of the colony, Edward M. Wingfield, was found guilty of libel and deposed. The only one who seemed to be able to keep any kind of order was John Smith. And he was captured by Indians and was fortunate to escape alive. The local Indians, put off by the attitudes of the colonists and recognizing the weakness of the newcomers, did not hesitate to attack them on many occasions.

The first winter was extremely cold. Only 38 remained of the original 105 colonists. The lack of preparation during the summer left them short of everything. Few supplies had arrived from England. At one point, Smith had to turn the fort's cannon on them to prevent them from taking the ship *Discovery* and returning to England.

The next two winters didn't see any improvement. There still was no production of any kind of store from the abundant resources available. The winter of 1609-1610 became known as the "Starving Time." They ate everything they had, even resorting in some cases, to cannibalism. Nearly 90 percent of the colony died that winter.

The reason for this starvation could be traced to the lack of willingness to work. Those who were lazy knew they could draw from the common store. Those who were willing to work got tired of supporting the lazy, so they didn't work as hard. The result was a lack of production and ultimately, starvation.

John Smith identified the problem in his *Generall Historie of Virginia*, in a section that summarized the writing of Ralph Hamor.

> *When our people were fed out of the common store, and laboured jointly together, glad was he could slip from his labour, or slumber over his taske he cared not how, nay the most honest among them would hardly take so much true paines in a weeke, as now for themselves they will doe in a day, neither cared they for the increase, presuming that howsoever the harvest prospered, the generall store must maintaine them, so that wee reaped not so much Corne from the labours of thirtie as now three or foure doe provide for themselves.*

A new governor, Sir Thomas Dale, arrived from England and he considered the situation so critical that he implemented martial law. The solution was simple. Every man was allotted three acres to clear and farm. They were henceforth to grow their own food. Of course, that meant that anyone who didn't work didn't eat.

The Pilgrims

The sponsors of the Jamestown expedition felt that the concept of communal ownership was very biblical, however. They were sure that the problem was in the lack of religious scruples among the colonists. If only a more spiritual company of people was to try it, they were sure the plan for the colony would succeed. Consequently, when they were approached by another group who wanted to move to America, they felt they could try it again.

The Pilgrims had already moved once. They left the religious persecution of England and settled in Holland where religious tolerance was much greater. They found that they were not happy there either because they felt their children were being corrupted by the loose morals of the Dutch. Plans were made to move to America where they could build a religious community that would be an example for the whole world to follow.

The problem was money. They had to find sponsors who would pay for the trip. After considerable negotiation, an agreement was reached in 1620. Under the auspices of the London Company, seventy London businessmen would engage in a seven-year joint-stock agreement with the Pilgrims. Much like the Jamestown colony, the Pilgrims were to have all things in common. All produce was to be put in a common store and everyone would draw their food equally from that stock.

Also like Jamestown, the Pilgrims nearly starved. And for the same reasons. The governor of the colony, William Bradford, described the laziness of the early settlers.

> *For the young men, that were most able and fit for labor and service, did repine that they should spend their time and strength to work for other men's wives and children without any recompense. The strong, or man of parts, had no more in division of victuals and clothes than he that was weak and not able to do a quarter the other could; this was thought injustice. The aged and graver men to be ranked and equalized in labors and victuals, clothes etc., with the meaner and younger sort, thought it some indignity and disrespect unto them. And for men's wives to be commanded to do service for other men, as dressing their meat, washing their clothes, etc., they deemed it a kind of slavery, neither could many husbands well brook it.*

In the spring of 1623, Bradford intentionally abandoned the agreement with the London merchants, and assigned everyone property. The result was an immediate increase in productivity.

> *And so assigned to every family a parcel of land, according to the proportion of their number, for that end, . . . and ranged all boys and youth*

*under some family. This had very good success,
for it made all hands very industrious, so as much
more corn was planted than otherwise would have
been by any means.*

The experience of the first two settlements in America confirmed the biblical principle that work is good.

*The person who labors, labors for himself,
For his hungry mouth drives him on.*
(Proverbs 16:26)

This is the heritage of America – hard work and self-sufficiency. When Thomas Jefferson penned those now famous words "the pursuit of happiness," and called it an unalienable right, he was essentially saying that we have the God-given right to work hard and to enjoy the security that comes from the fruit of our labor. Work is happiness.

---

[1]Fleming, *Now We Are Enemies*, pg. 52-53.
[2]Gross, *The Minutemen and Their World*, pg. 117-118.
[3]*Ibid.*, pg. 121.
[4]*Ibid.*
[5]*Ibid.*
[6]Bowen, *Miracle at Philadelphia*, pg. 71.
[7]*Ibid.*
[8]Ludwig, *Napoleon*, pg. 37.
[9]Bowen, *Miracle at Philadelphia*, pg. 70.
[10]Gross, *The Minutemen and Their World*, pg. 155.
[11]Bowen, *Miracle at Philadelphia*, pg. 72.
[12]*Ibid.*
[13]*Ibid.*

★★★★★

Individual Right #9

The Right To Hold An Opinion

★★★★★

Responsibility #9

Stand For Truth

★★★★★

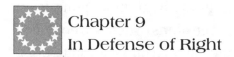

Chapter 9
In Defense of Right

Facts are stubborn things; and whatever may be our wishes, our inclination, or the dictates of our passions, they cannot alter the state of facts and evidence. (John Adams, in defense of the British Soldiers on trial for the Boston Massacre)

The American Revolution made no sense to most of those living in Great Britain. America prospered and the British believed it was primarily because British soldiers were stationed along the frontier to protect the colonies from the French and from the Indians. King George and the Parliament felt it was only fair that the colonists share in the expense involved in maintaining those troops. The king's chief minister stood in Parliament in 1763 and declared, "Great Britain protects America; America is bound to yield obedience."

It seemed simple enough. Just pass a few taxes to share the burden, crack down on illegal smuggling and everything would work out. The colonists, however, had gotten used to being beyond the reach of British government. It seemed like an encroachment from a foreign nation.

But the British set out to raise revenue from America and make sure the colonists knew their proper place in the British Empire. They established more efficient means of collecting taxes. They made efforts to stop smuggling, which resulted in the court cases where James Otis became well known. They tried to gain more control over trade. And the Americans resisted.

Most of the resistance in the beginning came from Boston. In 1768 a mob attacked customs officials who seized one of John Hancock's ships and charged him with smuggling wine. The escalation of violence resulted in 700 British troops marching into the town and establishing a kind of martial law. Boston began to feel like an occupied city. And in a sense it was.

Some of the colonists began conducting a sort of guerilla war against the occupiers. Groups known as the "Sons of Liberty" began meeting secretly and engaging in sometimes illegal activities. Customs officials were often tarred and feathered. They frequently feared for their lives. The British troops in Boston tried to protect them but the tension between soldiers and townspeople escalated until bloodshed was almost inevitable.

The degree to which colonial animosity affected relations between the soldiers and the city is demonstrated by the comment of a justice during a trial of a soldier from the 14th Regiment. He openly declared "that the soldiers must now take care of themselves,

> Some of the colonists began conducting a sort of guerilla war against the occupiers.

nor trust too much to their arms, for they were but a handful; that the inhabitants carried weapons concealed under their clothes, and would destroy them in a moment, if they pleased." The citizens were told that the soldiers were not allowed to fire at them under any circumstances, which made them even more brash and insulting.

On Friday March 2, 1770, an off-duty soldier walked into a ropewalk owned by a man named Samuel Gray. The British soldiers often supplemented their income by looking for odd jobs. The soldier asked if the rope makers had any extra work. One of them sneered at him, "Go clean my outhouse."

A fight ensued and the soldier, outnumbered, got the worst of it. He returned a little later with some of his friends and a brawl broke out. It ended without any serious injuries but the issue was not decided. One of the soldiers, Matthew Killroy, would meet Samuel Gray a few days later. Officials tried to smooth things over but resentment simmered on both sides.

The explosion came three days later. On the evening of March 5, a lone sentry named Hugh White stood guard at the entrance to the Boston Customs House. It was a snowy moonlit night. A young barber's apprentice named Edward Garrick shouted an insult at White. The British private tried to drive the boy off. In the scuffle, he struck Garrick in the ear with the butt of his musket. The young man ran off yelping for help. He returned with an unruly mob, mostly boys and youths, pointed at the lone sentry and shouted that he was the one who knocked him down.

Someone started ringing the bells in the nearby Old Brick Church, normally a signal that there was a fire. People poured into the streets looking for the flames. By nine o'clock there was a crowd of nearly a hundred people gathered around White.

Some began to throw snowballs and chunks of ice. The sentry, in self-defense, loaded his musket. The crowd dared him to fire. About twenty-five American sailors showed up, led by a man named Crispus Attucks. They were armed with wooden clubs and joined energetically in the taunting of the sentry, knowing that he had orders never to fire.

The soldier finally called for help. Captain Thomas Preston, the officer of the guard, appeared with a squad of six privates and a corporal. Matthew Kilroy, one of the soldiers in the earlier brawl, was in the squad. They marched with fixed bayonets to the Customs House, lined up facing the crowd and loaded their muskets.

The clamor drew more people until the mob was 300 to 400 strong, shouting, taunting, calling the soldiers "bloody backs" and "lobsters" and daring them to fire. Many threw snowballs, ice, oyster shells and lumps of coals. Crispus Attucks and other sailors pushed to the front and struck at the soldiers muskets with their clubs. Attucks himself kept shouting, "Kill them!" and "Knock them over!" They felt a certain amount of security because none of them believed that the British would fire.

From the back of the mob, someone threw a club that struck private Montgomery and knocked him to the ground. Furious, he jumped back to his feet and fired at Attucks who dropped dead.

The shot unleashed a flurry of fire from the other soldiers. Private Kilroy leveled his musket at Samuel Gray and killed him. The soldiers began to reload while Captain Preston frantically ordered them to stop firing. Three colonists lay dead and eight wounded, two of them mortally.

The crowd fell back. Some of them returned to help the wounded. The mob regrouped out of sight of the British and swore to kill all of the soldiers. Preston marched his men back to the barracks and called out the rest of the regiment.

The Governor of Massachusetts, Thomas Hutchinson, hurried to the Old State House. From a balcony he pleaded with the crowd to let the legal system work. "The law shall have its course. I will live and die by the law," he shouted at the mob. They finally dispersed.

The Trial

The incident became known in American history as the Boston Massacre. It turned into a murder trial that stirred the whole country. The next day, Samuel Adams led a huge protest that eventually resulted in Governor Hutchinson removing all British troops from the center of the city to a fortified island in the harbor. A week later, the colony's attorney general issued thirteen murder indictments. Three trials were held. The first was for Captain Preston. The second was for the other eight soldiers. A third trial was for four customs officers who were accused of shooting from the building. The third case was dropped when it was discovered the chief prosecution witness had falsely accused the customs officers.

Most Americans have heard of the Boston Massacre. We read something about it in history class, usually a paragraph or two that said the evil British killed five Americans and demonstrated their tyranny which got all of America excited and led to the Revolutionary War.

While it is true that the incident had a considerable impact on the development of resistance to Britain, we have not generally been told the whole story. The presence of British soldiers in Boston created an atmosphere that was almost guaranteed to explode into violence. It grew steadily for two years and it finally happened.

It is in the trial that we see the true character and courage of one of our Founding Fathers and an example that we should emulate. Captain Preston's trial began on October 24, 1770 and lasted for six days, a long time for a trial of that time. It had the kind of notoriety that we would associate today with the O.J. Simpson trial.

Preston could not find an attorney who would defend him. The colonists wanted to see all of the soldiers hanged and the way that the Sons of Liberty treated customs officials, anyone who acted on the behalf of the British would be risking his life. A Tory merchant spoke to a well-respected thirty-five year old lawyer named John Adams and convinced him to take the case.

John's cousin Sam Adams was furious with him, as were many of the Sons of Liberty. But Adams believed that it was vital that the British receive a fair trial or the very principles of unalienable rights would be completely compromised. He took the case. He was joined by a Tory judge named Robert Auchmuty and a young Patriot named Josiah Quincy.

The trial of Preston and later, the trial of the eight soldiers, had a couple of unusual twists. It was the first time a judge used the phrase "reasonable doubt." It came from Justice Peter Oliver:

> *If upon the whole ye are in any reasonable doubt of their guilt, ye must then, agreeable to the rule of law, declare them innocent.*

Hearsay testimony was allowed. Patrick Carr, one of the mortally wounded colonists, made statements just before he died that were allowed as evidence because it was felt that a man about to die would not lie.

Preston's case revolved on whether or not he gave an order to fire. Some witnesses said he did. Others claimed he was yelling "Don't fire." In the end, the jury decided that there was not enough evidence to convict and Preston was acquitted.

The trial for the eight soldiers started a month later. The prosecutors built a case based on the soldier's hatred for the colonists. Quincy opened for the defense by reminding the jury that the soldiers had to be judged on the basis of the evidence presented to the court and nothing else. The defense case rested on painting a picture of the circumstances that showed the soldiers fired in self-defense and not with the intention to murder.

Numerous witnesses were questioned. Dr. John Jeffries was the physician who attended to Patrick Carr, who died from his wounds. His testimony was important for the defense.

> *He told me . . . he was a native of Ireland, that he had frequently seen mobs, and soldiers called upon to quell them . . .. he had seen soldiers often fire on the people in Ireland, but had never seen them bear half so much before they fired in his life.*

When asked when his last conversation with Carr was, Dr. Jeffries replied:

> *About four o'clock in the afternoon, preceding the night on which he died, and he then particularly said, he forgave the man whoever he was that shot him, he was satisfied he had no malice, but fired to defend himself.*

Adams closed the defense arguments with the words, "the eight prisoners at the bar, had better be all acquitted, though we should admit them all to be guilty, than, that any one of them should by your verdict be found guilty."

Six of the soldiers were acquitted. Kilroy was found guilty of manslaughter for killing Samuel Gray and Montgomery was found guilty of manslaughter for killing Crispus Attucks. Both Kilroy and Montgomery pleaded "benefit of clergy," a Medieval law that allowed them to escape the death penalty. They were given a brand on their thumb and released.

It is the character and the courage of John Adams and Josiah Quincy that are notable in this story. They risked their reputations and their lives to defend the soldiers and they presented a clear enough case that most of their clients were exonerated. The results of the trials were accepted by the population with absolute calm.

It was a case of doing something that was politically incorrect for no other reason than because it was the right thing to do. It has become popular to say something like, "I may disagree with your opinion but I will defend to the death your right to express it." These words are often spoken for effect by people who probably would not actually do what they said. Adams and Quincy put those words into action. They defended their enemies against unjust accusations. In his diary, Adams made clear that he recognized what was at stake.

I have reason to remember that fatal Night. The Part I took in Defense of Captn. Preston and the Soldiers, procured me Anxiety, and Obloquy enough. It was, however, one of the most gallant,

generous, manly, and disinterested Actions of my
whole Life, and one of the best Pieces of Service I
ever rendered my Country. Judgement of Death
against those Soldiers would have been as foul a
Stain upon this Country as the Execution of the
Quakers or Witches, anciently. As the Evidence
was, the Verdict of the Jury was exactly right.

Mutiny of the Army

Standing for truth is often just a matter of courage, a willingness to risk reputation or popularity for the sake of doing what is right. That kind of determination and character is what makes great leaders. And great leaders are needed. The degree of influence that one man or woman of character and strength has on the course of the nation is tremendous.

George Washington was just such a leader. He was no more perfect than any of the other Founding Fathers and we do not want to give an unrealistic picture of him that makes him appear as a messianic character. He had faults. His temper, for example, was legendary.

During the retreat from Kips Bay on September 15, 1776, Washington could not get the fleeing soldiers to stop. At one point he managed to piece a line together but the appearance of a handful of British caused them to break and run without a shot being fired. The eruption of anger on that occasion started stories that circled the army for years. He struck several officers and at least three times threw his hat to the ground in disgust, finally lamenting, "Good God! Have I got such troops as those?" Aides had to lead his horse away to keep him from being captured.[1]

Early in the war, a fight broke out in camp between a New England unit and some Virginia riflemen. A young boy who was there remembered Washington in a fit of rage shaking riflemen as if they had been schoolboys as other men fled the scene to escape his wrath.[2] It was a lifelong problem. When Washington was sixteen an employer complained to his mother, "I wish I could say that he governs his temper."[3] Thomas Jefferson, who knew him well, wrote of Washington's temper.

> *His temper was naturally irritable . . . but reflection and resolution had obtained a firm and habitual ascendancy over it. If ever, however, it broke its bonds, he was most tremendous in his wrath.*[4]

One such incident that Jefferson witnessed occurred at a cabinet meeting when Washington "got into one of those passions when he cannot command himself."[5]

It is not our purpose to degrade George Washington. In fact we believe that he was one of the greatest leaders in American history. His life demonstrates the fact that great leaders are nothing more than ordinary men and women who rise to the challenge of circumstances. Washington had his problems. But he was there when he was needed and he stood for right even when it was not popular.

Most Americans are not aware of how close the Revolution came to failing because of the actions of Americans themselves. During one crisis, Washington stood nearly alone and prevented what could have been an irreparable disaster.

By 1783, the Revolution had been won. Cornwallis surrendered at Yorktown two years earlier and peace negotiations were under way. But the war was not over even though the fighting had virtually stopped. There were still armies in the field and Washington, along with many members of the Continental Congress, feared that their own troops would simply slip away too early and hand the country back to the British.

Congress had some serious problems that took up most of their time. In 1781, the states had all ratified the Articles of Confederation, the framework for the new government. There was such a great fear of a strong central government becoming tyrannical that the central government was forbidden to raise

Most Americans are not aware of how close the Revolution came to failing.

taxes. That authority remained in the hands of the state governments. Each was supposed to contribute a share of money for the Confederation government to meet its obligations.

Most of the state governments were slow to send money even when the fighting was in full swing. Now that peace was so near, almost nothing was forthcoming. By the summer of 1782, Congress had a mere $125,000 to cover $6 million of expenses. They could not even pay interest on loans.[6] A measure was proposed to allow the Congress to levy a 5 percent tax on goods imported into the country, but it required an amendment to the Articles of Confederation with the unanimous agreement of the states. Twelve said yes but Rhode Island refused and the Congress remained broke.[7]

The army was in an increasingly hostile mood. The soldiers had not been paid anything for many months. Some had pay due from as far back as four or five years. Three years earlier, Congress had made a promise of a life-time pension for those officers who agreed to stay with the army through the duration of the war. It started to look to them as though the states would never honor that agreement, a perception increased by the announcement that the allowance they received for meals was being reduced.[8] All of this came at a time when the countryside around them had supplied a plentiful harvest. The Continental Army lived in abject poverty in the midst of plenty.

The Continental Army lived in abject poverty in the midst of plenty.

The Congress was helpless to respond. Steps were taken to dismantle parts of the army so that the obligation of paying them could be avoided. On January 1, orders were given to consolidate many of the regiments, thus reducing the number of officers. Those not needed would be sent home without a penny.[9]

A delegation of officers traveled to the capital in January, 1783 to request some assurance that they would receive what they had been promised.[10] The delegation was led by Major General Alexander McDougall.[11] McDougall reported that many officers contemplated refusing to go home. They determined that their best hope was in remaining under arms until their demands were met.[12] It was a barely veiled threat of mutiny.

There was no hope of getting an amendment to the Articles of Confederation. Not only had Rhode Island refused to vote yes, but Virginia had withdrawn its ratification. In the crisis, several members of Congress launched themselves on a bizarre and dangerous path. Robert Morris, his assistant Gouverneur Morris, Alexander Hamilton, James Wilson and a number of others met with McDougall.[13] They encouraged his delegation to meet with various members of the Congress to paint for them as dire a picture as possible of the potential for the military marching on the capital. This was easy to do. McDougall only had to describe the truth. The efforts gained some sympathy but Congress stopped far short of what they had already promised.[14]

The next step was to encourage the officers to openly refuse to disband the army, even if the peace treaty was signed. An idea of how serious the matter was is indicated by the message that Gouverneur Morris took to Henry Knox. The conspirators knew Washington would never go along with their plan so they approached Knox, who had been with Washington through the entire war as chief of artillery. The army would trust him. Morris described what the army had to do.

The Army may now influence the legislatures and if you will permit me a metaphor from your own profession, after you have carried the post the public creditors will garrison it for you.[15]

Knox refused to be a part of the plan. These members of Congress were proposing nothing short of a military coup.

Everything that the Americans had fought for was opposed to the tyranny of a military control of government.

The man they finally approached was the second in command under Washington, General Horatio Gates. He was a man who had always felt somewhat slighted by being in Washington's shadow. He believed he should have been given the position of commander-in-chief. In late 1792, a group of young officers began to gather around Gates, believing that he would represent their complaints better than Washington. By January of 1793, Gates was in touch with members of the Congress.[16]

The conspirators encouraged Gates to resort to military action. On Monday, March 10, a notice was circulated around the camp that all officers should meet the next morning, ready to move beyond "meek language of entreating memorials." Gates was informed that the time had come for him to act.[17]

The conspirators did not want a revolt to succeed. They just wanted to scare the State governments enough to make them vote for changes in the Articles of Confederation. If a revolt got out of hand, the result would be a military dictatorship. Of course if they did nothing, disaster would result. It was a desperate gamble. They hoped to let it go far enough for that effect, but then somehow stop it before it went too far. The only one they felt could accomplish that was George Washington. Hamilton sent Washington an ambiguous warning, just enough to alert him so he would be ready to act, but without enough information to prompt him to bring a stop to it.[18]

It was on the 10th, when Washington read the notice being passed around, that he realized how serious the situation was. He was appalled at the prospect of the military taking the law into its own hands. That would be contrary to everything they had been trying to accomplish for the past decade.

Washington's first step was to gain time. He immediately sent out orders canceling the illegal Tuesday meeting and replaced it with another one on Saturday the 15th where officers could air their grievances. He made it appear that he would be away from the camp, which meant the meeting would be chaired by the ranking officer in the camp, Gates.[19]

The Meeting at New Windsor

Saturday morning arrived, one of the most dramatic and important moments in American history. The fate of the freedoms America stood for hung in the balance. The meeting took place at New Windsor in a log building constructed originally for religious services and social gatherings. It was a rectangle about forty by seventy feet with a platform at one end that served as a stage. Officers crammed into every space in the room. Gates stood up and opened the meeting.[20]

Suddenly, to everyone's surprise, George Washington walked into the room through a small door off the stage and walked to the platform. He asked to address the men. Gates really had no choice but to step aside.[21]

The audience was quietly hostile. Washington forcefully took the offensive. He expressed his "utmost horror and detestation" of anyone who would "open the flood gates of civil discord and deluge our rising empire in blood." He attacked the whole purpose of the meeting.

> *Let me entreat you gentlemen on your part not to take measures which, viewed in the calm light of reason, will lessen the dignity and sully the glory you have hitherto maintained.*[22]

The officers were quiet but not entirely convinced. Washington pulled a letter from his pocket that he said was from a member of Congress, expressing their concern for the plight of the soldiers. He tried to read it but he stumbled over the words, almost as though he could not read. Everyone in the hall strained to see what was wrong.

Washington reached into his pocket and pulled out a pair of spectacles. No one except his closest aides knew he needed them. He calmly said the words that brought every officer back to his sense of duty and a remembrance of the oath of loyalty when he joined the military.

> *Gentlemen, you will permit me to put on my spectacles, for I have not only grown gray but almost blind in the service of my country.*[23]

Washington read the letter but no one really heard anything he said. The imposing stature of the man, his personal courage, the sense of honor and duty that he conveyed along with the moment of human weakness that none of them were aware of combined to completely diffuse the situation. Many officers began crying, ashamed that they had even contemplated following the course of military action. Washington won them over by shear force of character.

He folded the letter and walked silently from the room, turning the meeting back over to Gates. Knox, placed in the meeting by Washington for this purpose, took advantage of the moment to propose a statement of thanks to the General. By the time it was finished, Gates and his friends were completely discredited.

In Congress, the near rebellion had the effect that the conspirators had wanted. The reluctant delegates were frightened enough to approve the measures needed to levy taxes and to pay the army. The gamble worked.

But the nearness of disaster cannot be overlooked. George Washington has been revered by Americans in every generation for a variety of legends and stories. Most Americans today know little about him except that he led the army of the Revolution and that he became the first president of the United States. They usually know a few stories like Washington chopping down the cherry tree or throwing the silver dollar across the Potomac.

In fact, both of these stories are fictitious and even the part about being the first president is technically not correct. There were other presidents before him, three of whom might qualify for the first president. The first government of the United States was the Continental Congress and the first president of that Congress in 1774 was Peyton Randolph. If you consider that the Congress did not think of itself as the government of an independent nation when it first met, then the beginning of the nation would be the signing of the Declaration of Independence. John Hancock was the president then. Or you might say that the government really began with the signing of the Articles of Confederation in 1781. The first president after that was John Hanson of Maryland. Washington himself referred to Hanson as the "President of the United States."[24]

These are not the things for which we should most remember Washington. Instead we ought to remember him for his courage in battle as demonstrated on numerous occasions, and above all, for his character and his devotion to principle, as demonstrated by this incident at the end of the war. Like Adams, Washington paid little attention to the odds against him or the political correctness of his actions. He was willing to take a stand simply because it was right. In doing so, he risked everything.

That is what made Washington and Adams true heroes in the history of America. That is why we should emulate them. In fact, we have a responsibility to do so.

[1]Scheer and Rankin, *Rebels and Redcoats*, pg. 205-206.

[2]Davis, *George Washington and the American Revolution*, pg. 44-45.

[3]Brookhiser, *Rules of Civility*, pg. 12, 14.

[4]Davis, *George Washington and the American Revolution*, pg. 23.

[5]Brookhiser, *Rules of Civility*, pg. 12, 14.

[6]Palmer, *1794*, pg. 5.

[7]*Ibid.*, pg. 6.

[8]*Ibid.*

[9]*Ibid.*, pg. 7.

[10]Davis, *George Washington and the American Revolution*, pg. 449.

[11]Palmer, *1794*, pg. 8.

[12]Scheer and Rankin, *Rebels and Redcoats*, pg. 579.

[13]Palmer, *1794*, pg. 9.

[14]*Ibid.*, pg. 10.

[15]*Ibid.*, pg. 11.

[16]*Ibid.*, pg. 12.

[17]*Ibid.*, pg. 13, and in Davis, *George Washington and the American Revolution*, pg. 450.

[18]Palmer, *1794*, pg. 13.

[19]*Ibid.*, pg. 16.

[20]*Ibid.*, pg. 17.

[21]*Ibid.*

[22]Scheer and Rankin, *Rebels and Redcoats*, pg. 580.

[23]Palmer, *1794*, pg. 18.

[24]Shenkman and Reiger, *One Night Stands With American History*, pg. 37.

★★★★★

Individual Right #10

The Right To Worship As You Choose

★★★★★

Responsibility #10

Tolerate Differences In Others

★★★★★

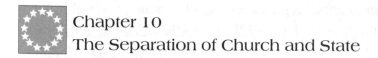

Chapter 10
The Separation of Church and State

. . . that truth is great and will prevail if left to herself, that she is the proper and sufficient antagonist to error, and has nothing to fear from the conflict, unless by human interposition disarmed of her natural weapons, free argument and debate, errors ceasing to be dangerous when it is permitted freely to contradict them. (Thomas Jefferson, "Statute for Establishing Religious Freedom," 1786)

On Thursday, November 13, 2003, Alabama's nine-member Court of the Judiciary issued a unanimous decision to remove Chief Justice Roy Moore from office. His offense was the defiance of a federal judge's order to remove a monument displaying the Ten Commandments from the rotunda of the state Supreme Court building. The whole issue sparked nation-wide controversy over the separation of church and state.

U.S. District Judge Myron Thompson ruled that the monument constituted a government endorsement of religion and therefore violated the First Amendment of the Constitution. Moore and his supporters claimed that the Ten Commandments are the foundation of the American legal system and the refusal to display them is a violation of the most basic principles of the Constitution.

Polls showed that 77 percent of Americans agreed with Moore. It has not been the only lawsuit concerning the Ten Commandments but it has certainly been the most publicized.

The story of Roy Moore really began several years earlier when he was a state court judge in Gadsden, Alabama. He placed a hand-carved plaque of the Ten Commandments in his courtroom and invited clergy to lead in prayer before trials.

Two different lawsuits were filed in March and April, 1995 with the support of the American Civil Liberties Union of Alabama to force Moore to remove the plaque. He won both cases.

The notoriety enabled Moore to run a highly visible campaign in 2000 for the office of Chief Justice. He became known as the "Ten Commandments Judge." He was elected on November 7 and took that victory as a mandate to continue his efforts to bring God back into the court system. He expressed his purpose in a speech the next year.

When I ran for the office of Chief Justice of the Alabama Supreme Court, I made a pledge to restore the moral foundation of law.

Shortly after the election, Moore met with a sculptor named Richard Hahnemann and attorney Stephen Melchior and, over eight months, designed the monument, a three-foot square, four-foot high granite block covered with inscriptions.[1]

The top of the monument featured two tablets angled in such a way that they gave the appearance of an open book sitting on a podium. The King James Bible Version of the Ten Commandments was engraved on the tablets. The sides of the granite cube featured fourteen other inscriptions. A larger quotation on each side was set apart in relief and smaller quotations relating to the same subject were place around the center.

The front of the monument featured a quote from the Declaration of Independence, "Laws of nature and of nature's God." It was surrounded with smaller quotes from George Mason, James Madison and William Blackstone about the relationship between nature's laws and God's laws.

The right side of the monument had "In God We Trust" surrounded by excerpts from the Preamble to the Alabama Constitution and the fourth verse of the National Anthem.

The left side had a quote from the Pledge of Allegiance, the 1954 version, "One nation under God, indivisible with liberty and justice for all." (The pledge was written in 1892 for the four-hundred-year anniversary of Columbus discovering America. "Under God" was not in the original. It was added in 1954.) Around it were smaller quotes from the legislative history of the pledge and from James Wilson and Thomas Jefferson, quotes that suggested that liberty and morality are based on God's authority.

The back of the monument had a large quotation from the Judiciary Act of 1789, "So help me God," with smaller quotes about oaths and justice by George Washington and John Jay.

This magnificent 2.6-ton sculpture was placed in the most conspicuous place in the Alabama Supreme Court building and dedicated by Judge Moore in a speech the next day. He left no doubt about his intentions.

This monument serves to remind the Appellate
Courts and the judges of the Circuit and District

Courts of this State and members of the bar who appear before them, as well as the people of Alabama who visit the Alabama Judicial Building, of the truth stated in the Preamble to the Alabama constitution that in order to establish justice we must invoke "the favor and guidance of Almighty God."

He spoke of the fact that the institutions of American society are founded on the belief that there is an authority and a moral law that transcends the State. He referred to principles that were espoused by our Founding Fathers. Rights come from God, not from government. He concluded with a declaration of his hope for Alabama and for America.

May this day mark the beginning of the restoration of the moral foundation of law to our people and a return to the knowledge of God in our land.

These noble aspirations didn't sit well with everyone, of course, and it wasn't long before civil actions were filed by three attorneys, Stephen Glassroth, Melinda Maddox and Beverly Howard. Unlike his previous court battles, however, Moore lost this one and he was ordered to remove the monument.

Even after the U.S. Supreme Court refused to hear the case, Moore defied the order and refused to move the monument. Hundreds of people rallied outside the court building to support Moore. Many were arrested. A week after the deadline issued by Judge Thompson, workers entered the building and removed the monument – and the federal court removed Moore.

Both sides claimed a constitutional basis for their position. Are the Ten Commandments the foundation of American law and is the restriction of their display an infringement of the freedom of speech? Or is the display of a religious text a violation of the Establishment Clause of the First Amend-ment? The debate over the Ten

Both sides claimed a constitutional basis for their position.

Commandments really revolves around just what the Constitution actually says. Before we can understand the Moore case in Alabama, we have to know the background of the First Amendment and the intentions of the Founding Fathers. We need to examine what they meant by separation of church and state.

The Danbury Baptists

The phrase "separation between church and state" never actually appears in the Constitution. It came from a letter that Thomas Jefferson wrote not long after his election as President in 1800. The letter was a response to the Danbury Baptist Association in Connecticut. The Baptists congratulated Jefferson on his victory and assured him of their support. They were excited by Jefferson's stand on religious freedom. It was something that they had been deprived of to a certain extent, even in a supposedly free America.

A huge portion of the early American settlers left England expressly for the purpose of finding a place where they could worship without restraint. Of course, the worship they had in mind was their own. In New England, it was the Puritans, who became the Congregationalist churches of the Revolutionary period. In Virginia, it was the Anglican Church. In the back country, it was the Presbyterians. Anyone else was persecuted. It was a freedom of worship as long as you worshiped the same way as the rest of the community.

As a result, most of the states had establishment churches. In Massachusetts, Connecticut and New Hampshire, for example, the Congregational Church was the official church sanctioned by the government. Salaries for clergy were paid by the State, not by the congregations. Tithes were more of a tax than a voluntary offering. Other denominations were required by law to pay tithes into the Congregationalist Church, whether they attended or not. A Baptist in Massachusetts or Connecticut found himself in the uncomfortable position of supporting a church he didn't like. This state of affairs had not changed much by the time of the Revolution. In 1774, at the time when charges of "taxation without representation" were being leveled at England from the colonists, Baptist Isaac Backus wrote to the Massachusetts legislature.

> *That which has made the greatest noise, is a tax of three pence a pound on tea; but your law of last June laid a tax of the same sum every year upon the Baptists in each parish. . . . And only because the Baptists in Middleboro' have refused to pay that little tax, we hear that the first parish in said town have this fall voted to lay a greater*

tax upon us. All Americans are alarmed at the tea tax; though, if they please, they can avoid it by not buying tea; but we have no such liberty. We must either pay the little tax, or else your people appear even in this time of extremity, determined to lay a greater one upon us. But these lines are to let you know, that we are determined not to pay either of them; not only upon your principles of not being taxed where we are not represented, but also because we dare not render that homage to any earthly power, which I and many of my brethren are fully convinced belongs only to God.[2]

The establishment church of Virginia was Anglican. The clergy were paid by the government. In fact, Patrick Henry first made a name for himself in Virginia politics by his involvement in a case known as the "Parson's Cause." It involved some Anglican ministers who claimed the parish tax collector owed them back wages.

The persecution was very real in most of the colonies. Roger Williams was kicked out of Massachusetts for religious differences. In 1651, a Baptist preacher named Obadiah Holmes went from Rhode Island to Massachusetts on a preaching mission. He was arrested in Boston, tried, convicted and whipped with thirty lashes.[3] Maryland began as a Catholic colony under Lord Baltimore. In the

★★★★★

Roger Williams was kicked out of Massachusetts for religious differences.

★★★★★

1640s, William Claiborne got control and every Jesuit that could be identified was expelled. Even an Act of Toleration in 1649 did not prevent the Catholics from being driven largely underground in the South.[4] A Separatist in Connecticut remarked that the Congregationalists were for peace "upon the same terms that the Pope is for peace, for he wants to rule over all Christians throughout the whole world."[5] These were not isolated incidents. Outside of Pennsylvania and Rhode Island, where religious toleration was given high priority, it was not easy to dissent from the established church. What made it so objectionable was that the persecution was not pagans attacking Christians. It was Christians attacking each other.

This is the context in which the Danbury Baptists wrote their letter to Thomas Jefferson. They didn't ask for anything in particular but they were happy that Jefferson was elected because they knew of his devotion to the cause of religious freedom.

Jefferson responded to the letter in what appears on the surface to be a simple thank you note. But he took the opportunity to make a statement about how he felt concerning religious coercion.

> *Believing with you that religion is a matter which lies solely between man and his God, that he owes account to none other for his faith or his worship, that the legislative powers of government reach actions only, and not opinions, I contemplate with sovereign reverence that act of the whole American people which declared that their legislature would "make no law respecting an*

establishment of religion, or prohibiting the free exercise thereof," thus building a wall of separation between Church and State.

Jefferson and the Baptists

It is doubtful that Jefferson expected his words to be as enduring as they have proven to be. But they did speak to his greatest passion in life. The Statute for Establishing Religious Freedom, passed in Virginia in 1786, along with the Declaration of Independence, were the only two things that Jefferson said he wanted to be remembered for. It resulted from a bill that Patrick Henry introduced into the Virginia Legislature that would have provided government sponsorship of Christian teachers. Jefferson opposed it vehemently.[6] More of his attention was devoted over a lifetime to religious freedom than any other topic. He certainly believed what he said.

The Danbury letter was published in Massachusetts about a month after it was sent and then forgotten until 1853, when it was published in a collection of Jefferson's writings. It was in 1878, however, that the famous phrase from that letter found its way into the legal system. In the Supreme Court case *Reynolds v. United States*, the court wrote "that it may be accepted almost as an authoritative declaration of the scope and effect of the [first] amendment."[7]

That was enough to make it stick. It became popular in 1947 and 1948, especially in *McCollum v. Board of Education*, a case involving whether or not religious education could be given in a public school. The court said, "in the words of Jefferson, the clause against establishment of religion by law was intended to erect a wall of separation between church and state."[8] Since then it is the phrase most often used to describe the intention of the Establishment Clause of the First Amendment.

Jefferson clearly thought his response to the Baptists was important. His election had been by a very narrow margin and one of the charges that his opponents had played up was his religious beliefs. He was accused of being an atheist because he was so determined to keep church and government separate. Where George Washington and John Adams, the two presidents before him, had regularly declared national days of prayer and thanksgiving, Jefferson adamantly refused to do so, believing that such proclamations were within the sphere of clergy, not presidents. Federalist preachers went so far as to declare from the pulpit that an epidemic of yellow fever that struck Philadelphia in 1799 was a divine punishment for the godlessness of Jeffersonian Republicans.[9] He knew that his letter to Danbury would be published and he saw it as an opportunity to clarify his position.

He wanted to issue a "condemnation of the alliance between church and state."

He received their letter on December 30, 1801 and wrote a first draft of his response immediately. He gave it to two New Englanders on his cabinet, Postmaster General Gideon Granger of Connecticut and Attorney General Levi Lincoln of Massachusetts. Jefferson told Lincoln that he wanted to accomplish two things with the letter. He wanted to issue a "condemnation of the alliance between church and state." And he wanted to use the opportunity for "saying why I do not proclaim fastings & thanksgivings, as my predecessors did."[10]

Lincoln especially was concerned that the letter would offend too many of the voters in New England so he suggested some changes. Seven lines were eliminated and the letter was sent. The original draft still exists, however, preserved by the Library of Congress. It reveals some of the intentions that Jefferson had when he wrote. The original draft called it a "wall of eternal separation between Church & State." But his next sentence, deleted from the final version, showed that his concern was not so much for the stamping out of religion as it was to prevent the kind of religious persecution that had been a part of American and European life for as long as there had been churches.

Congress thus inhibited from acts respecting religion, and the Executive authorized only to execute their acts, I have refrained from prescribing even those occasional performances of devotion, practiced indeed by the Executive of another nation as the legal head of its church, but subject here, as religious exercises only to the voluntary regulations and discipline of each respective sect, confining myself therefore to the duties of my station, which are merely temporal, be assured that your religious rights shall never be infringed by any act of mine.[11]

The only reason these comments were taken out of the letter was Lincoln's advice that New Englanders had long been accustomed to their government leaders proclaiming days of fasts and thanksgiving and to impugn the practice by calling it a relic of British tyranny would be politically disastrous. Jefferson agreed, but his intentions are seen in the original nevertheless. His only purpose was to prevent the persecution of any citizen because of what that person believed. He never intended that there be no contact whatsoever between Church and State. He intended that their religious rights never be infringed by an act of a government official.

In fact, just two days after Jefferson sent the letter to Danbury, he attended a church meeting in the House of Representatives where Massachusetts preacher John Leland was preaching. He attended those meetings regularly throughout his administration.[12] Apparently he didn't think there was a problem with that connection between the Church and the House of Representatives. Jefferson was not exactly an evangelical, born again Christian in the sense we use the term today, but he was no atheist either. His desire was to end the coercion of a government in matters of conscience and belief. He never believed for a moment that the influences of biblical principles should cease to influence the men who made up the government.

The First Amendment and the Supreme Court

The First Amendment to the Constitution, ratified on December 15, 1791, was designed to guarantee certain rights that individual citizens possess.

Congress shall make no law respecting an establishment of religion, or prohibiting the free exercise thereof; or abridging the freedom of speech, or of the press; or the right of the people peaceably to assemble, and to petition the Government for redress of grievances.

While the Amendment protects individual rights, it has been the Supreme Court that has defined just what that means. It has proven to be a matter that very few people can approach objectively. On the one hand are Christians who believe that government leaders should declare biblical values regardless of the beliefs of dissenters. On the other side are those who seek not only to prevent government officials from speaking publicly about their beliefs but they attempt to use the First Amendment to completely silence all religious expression in any public setting. We will see that neither position is within the intentions of the Founding Fathers.

Numerous cases have involved what has become known as the "Establishment Clause." The Supreme Court has generally been careful to try to find the intention of the First Amendment and apply it to each case. The case of *Everson v. Board of Education* in 1947 examined whether or not it was appropriate to give government financial aid to a parochial school to help pay for transportation of children to school. The Court established a connection between "aid" to religion and "establishment" of religion. It was felt that aiding children in receiving an education was not an endorsement of the religion that the school adhered to. The benefit to the religious institution was only indirect. The real beneficiaries were the children.[13]

Other cases added to the definitions. In *McCollum v. Board of Education* in 1948, religious teachers were being allowed to come onto public school property and teach religious classes. The Court declared that this was a violation of the First Amendment because it involved the use of public property for a religious purpose.

But in *Zorach v. Clauson*, just four years later, children were released from school with the permission of their parents so that they could attend religious classes off the campus. The Court ruled that this was not a violation of the Establishment Clause.

> *We are a religious people whose institutions presuppose a Supreme Being. We guarantee the freedom to worship as one chooses. We make room for as wide a variety of beliefs and creeds as the spiritual needs of man deem necessary. We sponsor an attitude on the part of government that shows no partiality to any one group and that lets each flourish according to the zeal of its adherents and the appeal of its dogma. When the state encourages religious instruction or cooperates with religious authorities by adjusting the schedule of public events to sectarian needs, it follows the best of our traditions. For it then respects the religious nature of our people and accommodates the public service to their spiritual needs.*

It was the 1971 case *Lemon v. Kurtzman* that provided what has become the test of constitutionality. Chief Justice Warren Burger explained the three-pronged requirement that is known as the "Lemon Test."

Every analysis in this area must begin with consideration of the cumulative criteria developed by the Court over many years. Three such tests may be gleaned from our cases. First, the statute must have a secular legislative purpose; second, its principal or primary effect must be one that neither advances nor inhibits religion, . . . finally, the statute must not foster "an excessive government entanglement with religion."

That last phrase came from a statement by James Madison, in his "Memorial and Remonstrance Against Religious Assessments" that a "prudent jealousy for religious freedoms required that they never become entangled." The Court has always recognized that a certain amount of entanglement is impossible to eliminate entirely. In the opinion from the Supreme Court case *Committee for Pub. Ed. v. Nyquist*, Justice Lewis F. Powell wrote:

Yet, despite Madison's admonition and the "sweep of the absolute prohibitions" of the Clauses, the Nation's history has not been one of entirely sanitized separation between Church and State. It has never been thought either possible or desirable to enforce a regime of total separation, and as a consequence cases arising under these Clauses have presented some of the most perplexing questions to come before this Court.

The intention was always to keep the spheres of civil activity and religious activity separated enough that government could not impose religious requirements on any citizens. It was never intended that government leaders cease being religious. There has always been a certain amount of overlap and there always will be. The only way to avoid it would be to prohibit religion entirely, and that would be a complete violation of the First Amendment.

John Locke on Toleration

We referred to John Locke in an earlier chapter as one of the primary influences on the Founding Fathers in their beliefs about how government should be structured. Locke was a devoutly religious man. He wrote an extensive treatise in 1689 called *A Letter on Toleration*. His thoughts on the subject give a good synopsis of what our Founding Fathers tried to encapsulate in the First Amendment. Locke considered at great length the separation of Church and State. He said that the magistrate's primary purpose was in the things of this world.

> *It is the duty of the civil magistrate, by the impartial execution of equal laws, to secure unto all the people in general and to every one of his subjects in particular the just possession of those things belonging to this life.*

The spiritual world was not a part of the magistrate's official responsibility and no magistrate should be allowed to impose his beliefs on others by law.

First, because the care of souls is not committed to the civil magistrate, any more than to other men. It is not committed unto him, I say, by God; because it appears not that God has ever given any such authority to one man over another as to compel anyone to his religion. Nor can any such power be vested in the magistrate by the consent of the people, because no man can so far abandon the care of his own salvation as blindly to leave to the choice of any other, whether prince or subject, to prescribe to him what faith or worship he shall embrace. For no man can, if he would, conform his faith to the dictates of another. All the life and power of true religion consist in the inward and full persuasion of the mind; and faith is not faith without believing. Whatever profession we make, to whatever outward worship we conform, if we are not fully satisfied in our own mind that the one is true and the other well pleasing unto God, such profession and such practice, far from being any furtherance, are indeed great obstacles to our salvation.

Just a few paragraphs later, however, Locke makes it clear that religious expression is entirely appropriate for a magistrate, as long as he does not use force to make his point.

It may indeed be alleged that the magistrate may make use of arguments, and, thereby draw the heterodox into the way of truth, and procure their salvation. I grant it; but this is common to him with other men. In teaching, instructing, and redressing the erroneous by reason, he may certainly do what becomes any good man to do. Magistracy does not oblige him to put off either humanity or Christianity; but it is one thing to persuade, another to command; one thing to press with arguments, another with penalties.

Even a government official has a right to religious expression. He is just not allowed to use his position in the government to impose his beliefs.

But, it may be asked, by what means then shall ecclesiastical laws be established, if they must be thus destitute of all compulsive power? I answer: They must be established by means suitable to the nature of such things, whereof the external profession and observation – if not proceeding from a thorough conviction and approbation of the mind – is altogether useless and unprofitable. The arms by which the members of this society are to be kept within their duty are exhortations, admonitions, and advices.

The gospel was never meant to be forced on anyone. It is to be spread through love. Locke questioned how effective coercion could ever be in demonstrating the right attitude of a Christian.

For it will be very difficult to persuade men of sense that he who with dry eyes and satisfaction of mind can deliver his brother to the executioner to be burnt alive, does sincerely and heartily concern himself to save that brother from the flames of hell in the world to come.

It was the principle of toleration that the Founding Fathers, especially Jefferson and Madison, sought to establish in the new nation. It was the fear that any group, no matter how well meaning, if given unrestrained power over another, would become dictatorial. As Abigail Adams wrote to her husband, "Remember, all men would be tyrants if they could." Instead, America would become a nation that would, in the words of a Jewish congregation in Newport, "give to bigotry no sanction, to persecution no assistance."[14]

The Godless Constitution

It is interesting to see the degree of resistance to the Constitution precisely because it did not contain any reference to God. There was a public outcry that this new Constitution did not affirm any faith, not even Christianity in general. It had no acknowledgement of God. It did not even require government officials to declare a belief in God. One opponent of the Constitution in New Hampshire declared that "a Turk, a Jew, a Roman Catholic, and what is worse than all, a Universalist, may be President of the United States."[15] The multitudes were convinced that this atheistic government was doomed to divine judgment.

The federal government left much to the states. Most state constitutions contained references to God. Often it was a reaction to the total absence of such language in the United States Constitution. It was the "capital defect" in the words of

Samuel Austin. To Congressman Samuel Taggert, it was "a national evil of great magnitude."[16] In the nineteenth century, a group was formed under the name of National Reform Association. Their task was to get the Constitution rewritten to reflect the Christian foundation of the nation. They proposed a new preamble.

> *Recognizing Almighty God as the source of all authority and power in civil government, and acknowledging the Lord Jesus Christ as the Governor among the nations, His revealed will as the supreme law of the land, in order to constitute a Christian government, we the people . . ."*

The recorded arguments of the time indicate that the National Reform Association represented the views of the vast majority of Americans. Yet the Founding Fathers and other government leaders never changed their minds. Religious freedom, freedom of conscience, did not mean freedom to believe in the Christian god. It meant freedom to believe in the Christian god, the Muslim god, the gods of paganism or no gods.

One of the most famous statements by Thomas Jefferson is carved on the Jefferson Memorial in Washington D.C. "I have sworn upon the altar of god, eternal hostility against every form of tyranny over the mind of man."

These words were written in reference to this issue of state-supported churches. In a letter to Benjamin Rush in 1800, Jefferson complained that the Federalist clergy of New England opposed his candidacy for president because they still hoped to have a national religion and they knew he would oppose it. He saw the establishment of a state-supported religion as a tyranny over the mind, an attempt to remove the personal responsibility of every person to think for himself.

> *They believe that any portion of power confided to me will be exerted in opposition to their schemes. And they believe truly. For I have sworn upon the altar of god, eternal hostility against every form of tyranny over the mind of man.*

To Jefferson, "tyranny over the mind of man" was a state supported church. Against great opposition, the states all finally disenfranchised the state churches. It didn't happen immediately after the ratification of the Constitution. It was a matter left to the states. Connecticut didn't vote to let the church go until 1818. Theologians and preachers all over the country predicted that America would fall into apostasy and judgment. It looked like the end of America as a Christian nation.

Preachers all over the country predicted that America would fall into apostasy and judgment.

In fact, exactly the opposite happened. Lyman Beecher, a Congregationalist minister in Connecticut, expressed the essence of what became a time of great revival. He was adamantly and actively opposed to the move to disenfranchise the state church.

It was a time of great depression and suffering. It was the worst attack I ever met in my life, . . . I worked as hard as mortal man could, and at the time preached for revivals with all my might . . . till at last, what with domestic afflictions and all, my health and spirits began to fail. It was as dark a day as ever I saw. The odium thrown upon the ministry was inconceivable. The injury done to the cause of Christ, as we then supposed, was irreparable. For several days I suffered what no tongue can tell for the best thing that ever happened to the State of Connecticut. It cut the churches loose from dependence on state support. It threw them wholly on their own resources and on God.[17]

They threw their dependence on God. It was such a unique concept that it stunned people. Imagine a church whose reliance was on God and not on the state. Over the next fifty years, churches began to recruit volunteers to do the work of ministry that had previously been done by government employees. Pastors could no longer count on the State forcing the congregation to give money. They now had to make the congregation believe in the mission of the church on this earth. They had to actually excel at what they did. If they did not preach well, people would simply go somewhere else.

It was during this time that America saw an explosion in church work and church expansion. Bible societies were formed. Sunday School was invented. Missions were organized. The movement to eliminate slavery took on a completely different tone. America became the first society in history to eliminate slavery for non-economic reasons. We banned it for no other reason than because it was wrong. Laymen and laywomen became the driving force in the spiritual life of America. The nation of the people developed a church that was of the people as well. The revival known as the Second Great Awakening swept the nation.

The observant Frenchman, Alexis de Tocqueville, noted in the 1830s how far Christianity had come.

> *I do not know whether all Americans have a sincere faith in their religion – for who can search the human heart? – but I am certain that they hold it to be indispensable to the maintenance of republican institutions.*

He made this statement at a time when the absence of religious expression in the Constitution was supposed to have doomed America to the wrath of God. It seems that the less "Christian" the government became, the more "Christian" the nation was. We are convinced that the same principle holds true today. When the people of God devote their energies to the work of the ministry, the nation remains Christian simply because the people are Christian.

We have begun to wonder if the non-profit status that churches enjoy is not more of a hindrance than a help to the preaching of the gospel. Are we dependent on the favors of the Internal Revenue Service for the success of our ministries or are we dependent on God? Does the survival of Christianity in America depend on displaying the Ten Commandments in our courtrooms or does it depend on the principles of the Ten Commandments being demonstrated in the lives of God's people? Does the salvation of the lost depend on having God mentioned in the Preamble to the Constitution or does it depend on the prayer and the testimony of believers?

This does not mean that we should not be active in the political arena. A Christian is more likely to make morally correct decisions that are based on a biblical worldview than a non-Christian. Neither does it mean that every decision made by the Supreme Court will uphold the real intentions of the Founding Fathers. We saw ample evidence of that in the Dred Scott Case.

★★★★★

It does not prevent a government official from proclaiming his faith.

★★★★★

But it does mean that the wall of separation between church and state is not a bad thing when it is understood in its original context. It was intended to prevent government from imposing on the rights of a citizen to believe and to worship according to his own conscience. It does not prevent a government official from proclaiming his faith nor does it prevent him from trying to convince others of his belief through persuasion or argument. He has this right by virtue of his existence as a human being. Public office does not require him to lay it aside. The separation of church and state also requires that we depend on God, not on the state.

The Lemon Test in Alabama

With these principles of the First Amendment in mind, we can return to the story of Judge Moore and the Ten Commandments Monument. Judge Thompson and the other eight judges in the case ruled unanimously that Moore be ordered to remove the Ten Commandments Monument from the Alabama Supreme Court building. As you recall, Judge Moore defied the order and the Court then removed him from his office. There are a couple of observations that we can make about the direction that the case took. They have not usually been addressed in the media reports that we have seen.

First of all, we recognize that most of our readers will agree with us that it is a sad comment on the state of our society that the display of the Ten Commandments should be prohibited anywhere. But in fairness to Judge Thompson, we must say that there are some other elements to this case that have not been included much in the conversation by either side. The public debate has centered almost exclusively on the Ten Commandments.

This is actually somewhat odd, since, on the issue of displaying the Ten Commandments, both sides in the case seemed to agree. In his opinion, issued in November 2002, Judge Thompson explained the reasons for the court's unanimous decision. And it is interesting that he begins his comments by agreeing with the idea of the Ten Commandments being posted in public places.

> *But, in announcing this holding today, the court believes it is important to clarify at the outset that the court does not hold that it is improper in all instances to display the Ten Commandments in government buildings; nor does the court hold that the Ten Commandments are not important, if not one of the most important, sources of American law.*

Later in the document, Thompson admits the reasons why a religious document like the Ten Commandments can also serve a secular purpose.

> *To be sure, "The Ten Commandments are undeniably a sacred text in the Jewish and Christian faiths, and no legislative recitation of a supposed secular purpose can blind us to that fact." . . . But, as the evidence in this case more than adequately reflected, the Ten Commandments have a secular aspect as well. Experts on both sides testified that the Ten Commandments were a foundation of American law, that America's founders looked to and relied on the Ten Commandments as a source of absolute moral standards.*

The problem for the judges in the case was not the Ten Commandments. It was the other inscriptions on the monument, the words used by Judge Moore to dedicate the monument and the manner in which it was displayed.

> *The court appreciates that there are those who see a clear secular purpose in the Ten Commandments, for they command not only such things as "I am the Lord thy God" and "Thou shalt have no other Gods before me" but also, among other things, that "Thou shalt not kill" and "Thou shalt not steal," and that we should "Honour thy father and thy mother." If all Chief Justice Moore had done were to emphasize the Ten*

Commandments' historical and educational importance (for the evidence shows that they have been one of the sources of our secular laws) or their importance as a model code for good citizenship (for we all want our children to honor their parents, not to kill, not to steal, and so forth), this court would have a much different case before it. But the Chief Justice did not limit himself to this; he went far, far beyond.

The problem was that the monument did not fit any of the criteria given in the "Lemon Test." In Thompson's words:

That Chief Justice Moore's purpose in displaying the monument was non-secular is self-evident. First, it is self-evident from his own words . . . He saw the placement of the monument in the Judicial building rotunda as not only "the beginning of the restoration of the moral foundation of law to our people," but, more fundamentally, as "a return to the knowledge of God in our land."

In his trial testimony before this court, the Chief Justice gave more structure to his understanding of the relationship of God and the state, and the role the monument was intended to play in conveying that message. He explained that the Juedeo-Christian god reigned over both the church and the state in this country, and that both owed allegiance to that God.

Moore testified that the design and arrangement of the monument reflected his understanding of the relationship between God and the state.

The second point in the "Lemon Test" was that the action could neither endorse or prohibit religion. Judge Thompson wrote that the monument failed to pass this test as well.

> Both in appearance and in stated purpose, the Chief Justice's Ten Commandments monument is an "extreme case"; it is nothing less than "an obtrusive year-round religious display" installed in the Alabama State Judicial building in order to "place the government's weight behind an obvious effort to proselytize on behalf of a particular religion," the Chief Justice's religion.

The third point in the "Lemon Test" is whether or not an excessive entanglement was created between the state and a religion. While Thompson did not directly make that point a part of his argument, in a footnote he did point out that the funding for much of Judge Moore's legal expenses came through a ministry called Coral Ridge, headed by Dr. James Kennedy. Coral Ridge used the publicity of the court case to raise contributions. Judge Moore was a frequent guest of Dr. Kennedy on the Coral Ridge Hour broadcast. Enough involvement was obvious that Thompson felt a case could be made that there was entanglement if anyone wanted to do so.

This is a very brief summary of the points made by Judge Thompson. Numerous times he stated that religious belief was appropriate but he concluded, along with the other eight judges on the case, that Judge Moore exceeded the limitations of the First Amendment in the manner that the monument was created and displayed.

> *Thus, the court stresses that it is <u>not</u> disagreeing with Chief Justice Moore's beliefs regarding the relationship of God and the state. Rather, the court disagrees with the Chief Justice to the extent that it understands him to be saying that, <u>as a matter of American law</u>, the Judeo-Christian God must be recognized as sovereign over the state, or even that <u>the state</u> may adopt that view.*

The Rule of Common Sense

Given the definitions by which the Supreme Court has judged the roles of church and state, it is hard to argue with the decision against Judge Moore. Having said that, however, there are some aspects of his position that need to be recognized as warnings concerning the direction our society is moving. The court usually deals with the letter of the law and the result does not always get to the heart of the matter.

A couple of things about the whole trial are a little troubling. The first is the fact that there was a case at all. It is not legally sufficient for a plaintiff to merely dislike something. He has to show that he has "standing," meaning that he must be able to show that he personally has suffered some actual or threatened injury. In Judge Thompson's opinion on the case, he addressed that fact.

> *To have standing to challenge a display under the Establishment clause, the plaintiffs must*

suffer personal injury "as a consequence of the alleged constitutional error, other than the psychological consequence presumably produced by observation of conduct with which one disagrees.

He defines the parameters of such an injury, essentially saying that it makes the plaintiff upset.

An "effect on an individual's use and enjoyment of public land is a sufficient noneconomic injury to confer standing to challenge governmental actions." ACLU of Georgia v. Ragun County Chamber of Commerce, Inc.

Thomas Jefferson, whose words are quoted in defense of every separation of church and state argument, also defined injury. He expressed his opinion in *Notes on the State of Virginia.*

The legitimate powers of government extend to such acts only as are injurious to others. But it does me no injury for my neighbor to say that there are twenty gods, or no God. It neither picks my pocket nor breaks my leg.[18]

The whole motivation seems to be questionable from the standpoint of mere common sense. While the tone of Judge Moore's monument was a violation of the First Amendment, the claim that it caused injury is no more rational than the Supreme Court's ruling that a pregnant woman has a legitimate right to end a human life because the pregnancy might delay her college education or her career. If lawsuits were filed over everything done and said by politicians that was objectionable to anyone else, there would be no more government. They would all have to be removed from office.

The other observation is that we believe it is not coincidental that the Supreme Court rulings that have delineated how the First Amendment should be applied began at about the same time that forced schooling was making dramatic changes in the education system of America. *Everson v. Board of Education* was in 1947. *McCollum v. Board of Education* was in 1948. *Zorach v. Clauson* was in 1952. *Lemon v. Kurtzman* was in 1971. *Committee for Pub. Ed. v. Nyquist* was in 1973.

As we noted in chapters 3 and 4, one of the goals of forced schooling was to separate people from the values of an earlier day. The Supreme Court definitions of the Establishment Clause are at the very least a direct reflection of that trend. They have taken what was intended to be a protection of the freedom to worship in your own way and turned it into a mandate to allow no public expression of worship at all. In the courts eyes, only non-Christians can be offended. The rulings do not take into account the offense directed at Christians by atheism and humanism, which are as much religious beliefs as Christianity or Islam. The courts have not considered the fact that teaching humanism in a school setting is as much religious instruction as a Bible study since it has a direct influence on religious beliefs of the student.

There is a spiritual struggle to silence the voice of Christians in America. The First Amendment, and for that matter, Jefferson's own words concerning separation of church and state, were never intended to force religion out of America. It was recognized that any government support of a particular religious group would eventually result in the persecution of everyone not in that group, regardless of the intentions of those who started it. Human nature has proved throughout history that persecution will happen. To ban religious expression is to put those who are anti-religion in a position of power where they can persecute those who have religious belief.

The First Amendment was designed to keep government out of church, not church out of government.

The First Amendment was designed to keep government out of church, not church out of government. It was never felt for one second by the Founding Fathers, not even Jefferson or Madison, that church would cease to have an influence on government. To use the First Amendment as an excuse to eliminate the influence of the church is a much greater violation of the First Amendment than any Ten Commandments display could ever be.

---

[1] Details of the monument and the display are taken from Judge Myron Thompson's Opinion, issued at the close of the trial.

[2] Gaustad, *Neither King Nor Prelate*, pg. 33.

[3] *Ibid.*, pg. 24.

[4] *Ibid.*, pg.29.

[5] *Ibid.*, pg. 31.

[6] Leahy, *The First Amendment*, 1791-1991, pg. 46.

[7] Library of Congress Information Bulletin, June 1998.

[8] *Ibid.*

[9]*Ibid.*

[10]*Ibid.*

[11]*Ibid.*

[12]*Ibid.*

[13]Leahy, *The First Amendment, 1791-1991*, pg. 46.

[14]Gaustad, *Neither King nor Prelate*, pg. 113.

[15]*Ibid.*

[16]*Ibid.*, pg. 118.

[17]*Ibid.*, pg. 120.

[18]*Ibid.*, pg. 42-43.

★★★★★

Individual Right #11

The Right To Safety

★★★★★

Responsibility #11

Influence The World

★★★★★

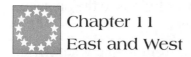

Chapter 11
East and West

I would rather be exposed to the inconveniences attending too much liberty than to those attending too small a degree of it. (Thomas Jefferson)

Film director Phil Cooke tells of shooting a documentary that required contacting a primitive tribe in the jungles of Brazil, near the headwaters of the Amazon.[1] He took a three-man crew with as much equipment as they could carry. They flew into the closest city to their destination that had an airport. From there, they chartered a small plane to fly them as far into the jungle as they could get. They had so much equipment that Phil had to sit on an oil can to fit into the plane. They were so loaded down that they could barely get off the ground. They even clipped a tree as they flew four hours to a remote dirt airfield. From there, they transferred to a freighter to continue up the Amazon. After an eight to ten-hour trip, the river narrowed so much that they had to change to canoes. Another day of travel brought them to their destination, a primitive village of thatched huts.

Phil had been warned that they should not enter the village unless invited, since those who did were usually killed. But the village looked completely deserted. They carefully made their way from hut to hut, looking for some sign of life, worried that they were walking into an ambush. Finally, they came to a hut at the far end of the village jammed full of natives, sitting shoulder to shoulder, their attention riveted on something at the front of the crowd, oblivious to the presence of the film crew.

As Phil made his way to the front to see what it was that held their attention so strongly, he found a beat up old black and white television hooked up to a car battery. This primitive tribe, several days' journey from the nearest civilization, was watching "Dallas."

The influence of the Western world, and the United States in particular, is astounding. You can go almost anywhere and you will find evidence of it. In the most remote desert or jungle area, you can find people wearing American baseball caps and blue jeans. Dinesh D'Souza comments on the irony of the 1970s heavyweight title fight between Muhammad Ali and George Foreman, held in the African nation of Zaire. Both Ali and Foreman strutted off the plane dressed in traditional African costumes complete with headdresses, and dashikis, trying to connect to their African roots. The crowd of natives that met them was dressed in suits and ties.[2]

Much of this influence is directly attributable to American media. Television and film have created a tremendous impact on other cultures. The television in the Amazon jungle is not an isolated incident. Everyone wants to tune in to American productions. Every film producer in America knows that at least sixty percent of a film's gross earnings will come from foreign markets.[3] It is noteworthy that after American troops gained control of the major cities in Afghanistan, nothing was operating. The first public function to reopen was not a hospital or a government office. It was the movie theatre.[4]

There are numerous reasons for this influence. In *What's So Great About America*, D'Souza identifies three areas in which the Western world was different than other parts of civilization and which created the enormous gap between the wealth of the West, Europe and America, and everyone else. The first, he believes, was the development of science, which gave us the technological advances that have made life so much better.

This has resulted in Western culture "conquering" the world.

Second was the development of democracy, which has empowered people to choose their own destiny instead of being forced into a chosen career or life pattern. The third was the development of capitalism that made the great affluence of the West possible. With affluence came time away from work and that made other pursuits possible that could improve life.

Over the past five hundred years, this has resulted in Western culture "conquering" the world in a way that no military empire has ever been able to. It is the conquest of ideas. No matter how much various cultures say that they do not want Western influence, they still try to bring in some aspect of it, usually through technology that they desire. The quality of life in the West is just so much better than anywhere else.

Of course, any culture could have developed those areas of superiority, but only the Western nations actually did. Historian David B. Ralston speaks of the "restlessness" of the West.

How Europe was able to establish its world hegemony is not something for which an explanation is necessarily self-evident. As of 1500, when this phenomenon was just getting under way, the Europeans enjoyed no significant advantages vis-à-vis other major civilizations, at least not in respect to their numbers, their technology, or their accessible natural resources. What they did seem to have was an innate restlessness, a perpetual dissatisfaction, that, despite custom and tradition, led them to look upon existing situations as "phenomena that not only could but should be changed."[5]

One of the primary accusations against the West is that we have gone into poor Third World countries and stolen all of their natural resources. The truth is that those nations were doing nothing with those resources and the presence of Western industry to develop them has been the main reason most countries have improved their standards of living over the past couple of centuries. Without the West, most would be even worse off than they are now. History has demonstrated that the overall mindset of most cultures is opposed to change and to development. Progress is a uniquely Western concept.[6] So often, other cultures have a kind of fatalistic attitude toward life. Whatever happens will happen.

In the documentary, "Desert Sky," Captain Eric Simon, who spent a year in Iraq with the 159th Aviation Assault Brigade, tells of the frustration of working with local contractors who had very little concern over deadlines or efficient delivery of building materials. When asked when needed supplies would arrive, they consistently replied, "Insha Allah," which means "God willing." It never seemed to occur to them that anything could be done to speed up the process. The difference in Western thinking stands in stark contrast and helps explain why so much more gets accomplished by American business.

Among the Western nations, the United States has risen to a level of dominance unlike anything in history. It has brought about the hatred of much of the rest of the world. Americans appear rich and arrogant. And they are rich. The poorest Americans live better than most of the rest of the world. During the 1980s, CBS broadcast an anti-Reagan documentary called "Poor Like Us." It was supposed to show the miseries of poor Americans during the recession. The Soviet Union, thinking to embarrass Reagan, carried the broadcast. It backfired. The average citizen of Russia discovered that even the poorest American had a television, a microwave and a car, things that they, the average Russian, just dreamed about.[7]

We thus find ourselves in a situation where America is the most blessed nation on earth but also the most hated. We need to understand why this is so. We are under attack from numerous sources and if we do not understand why, then we will find it difficult to defend ourselves. The truth of the matter is that much of the hatred of America is deserved.

The Hatred of America

It is not just a matter of jealousy, as so many Americans would like to think. While jealousy might be the primary reason Europeans hate America, especially the French, there are other factors that influence the way the rest of the world sees us.

D'Souza refers to the "Asian school" as one group that hates us.[8] It is mostly centered around the perception that America has succeeded in prosperity, technology and business but has become morally degenerate in the process. The Asian school seeks to take only part of what America has to offer, that is, to acquire the technology without taking the American culture, and by default, the American immorality. Lee Kuan Yew, the former prime minister of Singapore, calls it "modernization without Westernization."[9]

Everyone wants American technology but no one wants America. At least no government wants American influence. The citizens of other nations generally seem to want to move here to give them a chance for a better life. But even then they try to keep their old ways. Invariably they find that they cannot completely succeed. They have to change just because of the contact.

By far, the greatest challenge to America is the hatred that comes from the world of Islam. The problem is that the very concepts of Islam are diametrically opposed to the most cherished concepts of America. Islam teaches a theocracy. America is a republic. In a Muslim society, the Qur'an is the law and it is interpreted by the religious leaders. In America, the secular government is prevented from dictating religious practice. In a Muslim society, those who believe differently are severely restricted. In America, we teach that the individual has a right to believe what he wants. We encourage minority expression almost to the point of lunacy. In a Muslim society, those who argue against the religious rule are executed or imprisoned. In America we cherish freedom of speech.

Americans usually have a difficult time appreciating just how all encompassing these differences are.

Understanding them will help us to see why Islamic extremists are so intent on killing us.

As we noted earlier, America is more of an idea than it is a race or a geographical entity. While there are distinct boundaries to the nation called the United States, it is the principles of Natural Law and individual rights that set America apart. No other nation in history has had such an obsessive devotion to the liberty of the individual.

Of course, liberty also means that people are free to make choices – another thing that makes America unique. And logically, the freedom to make choices also means the freedom to make bad choices. There is a lot of garbage that goes with liberty.

That is the part that so enrages most of America's enemies. Islam is a religious system that focuses on external behavior. The word "Islam" means "submission," a submission to the rule of Allah. When Muslims look at America, they see licentious and immoral behavior that is completely contrary to their religious beliefs. The last thing that they want is to have that immorality contaminate their own countries. Where the Asian school tries to gain some things from

Freedom to make choices also means the freedom to make bad choices.

America that will improve the quality of life while rejecting the moral values of America, Islam recognizes that the concepts of the liberties of America cannot be entirely separated from any other part of America. Progress itself, being such a Western idea, is a dangerous thing to the lifestyles of Muslim countries.

When we look at the things that traditional Muslims accuse us of, it is hard to argue with them. They view us as being only interested in money. We are very materialistic. Yet we have seen that the work ethic inherent in the phrase "pursuit of happiness" is very much concerned with material wealth. We noted that capitalism is one of the elements that explain America's success but capitalism can easily lead to materialism and that is what the Muslim world sees.

Materialism is completely contrary to the precepts of Islam. There are many in the world of Islam who have great wealth but most of them use it differently than Americans. Osama bin Laden is worth millions of dollars but for the past several years, he has chosen to live in caves because of what he believes. His wealth has been committed to his cause. Yasser Arafat accumulated millions of dollars, yet he chose for many years to commit his wealth to the cause he believed in. Even the wealthiest of Islamic extremists cannot be accused of being materialistic in the sense that most Americans are. And even the most non-materialistic Americans have trouble understanding that.

Along with the wealth, there is a tendency for Americans to look down on those who do not have as much. We know we have achieved wealth through our efforts and we tend to think that anyone who wants to work can accomplish the same thing. Most Americans think of Muslims as lazy and uneducated. In reality, they are not. But they do live by very different standards than Americans. When they think of us, they do not perceive progress. Instead, they see arrogance.

In Muslim countries, women are required to wear veils. In America, women often wear close to nothing. American film and television portray an attitude toward sexual matters that runs completely contrary to what Muslims consider to be holy. They perceive America as a nation of loose morals and degradation. It is hard to argue with them.

Sayyid Qutb, Islamic philosopher from Egypt, identified what he considered to be so evil in the West. He believed that the West always separated the realm of God from the realm of society. Because of that, the two are bound to come into conflict with each other.[10] Qutb claimed that in the West, people still go to church and profess a religious belief but it is kept relatively separate from the secular realm and no longer has a shaping influence on society. In Islamic thinking, there is no real difference between the secular and the religious. Allah rules through the religious leaders. The American concept of separation of church and state is unthinkable to a traditional Muslim.

Of course this means that the population in a Muslim country is restricted to at least an outward show of Islamic belief. Everything that we have discussed regarding the freedom of conscience and the right to believe as the individual wants to, without coercion, is completely the opposite of the Islamic ideal.

It is not difficult, given these fundamental differences in beliefs, to see why so many Muslims hate us. Just as America is an idea, Islam, in recent years, has also become more of an idea than a nation. In the 1960s, the world saw the beginning of a form of religious allegiance to the Qur'an that placed the role of Islam above any national identity. Leaders such as Qutb, Mawdudi in Pakistan and Khomeini in Iran, proclaimed an ideology that Muslims everywhere could rally to.[11] It portrayed Islam as a religious belief that transcended national boundaries.

Khomeini demonstrated that he did not believe that his concept of Islam had any national boundaries when he issued the famous *fatwa* against Salman Rushdie, the author of *Satanic Verses*. By passing a death sentence against a man living in a Western nation, Khomeini made it clear that the decrees of Allah, as interpreted through himself, should reach to any part of the world.[12]

Before we make a wholesale condemnation of all Muslims, however, we must distinguish between some different types of Islamic belief. Just as Christianity contains numerous denominations that are really quite different from each other, there are many differences between the various Muslim groups. Unfortunately, most Americans make little or no distinction.

In the West, there are many Muslims, probably the majority, who have learned to appreciate the principles that America stands for. They value the individual rights that we have come to cherish and they live within those same freedoms. Tariq Ramadan has devoted much time and effort to defining the future of Western Muslims. In his book, *Western Muslims and the Future of Islam*, he makes a distinction between Eastern and Western based not only on the location but also on the efforts of Muslims to assimilate themselves into the societies in which they live.

We are currently living through a veritable silent revolution in Muslim communities in the West: more and more young people and intellectuals are actively looking for a way to live in harmony with their faith while participating in the societies that are their societies, whether they

like it or not. . . . Far from media attention, going
through the risks of a process of maturation that
is necessarily slow, they are drawing the shape of
European and American Islam: faithful to the
principles of Islam, dressed in European and
American cultures, and definitively rooted in
Western societies.[13]

But that is Western Muslims. It is safe to say that for those who adhere to the ideas of individual rights, they are already affected by the concepts of Western thinking. To a Muslim in one of the traditional Islamic cultures, such assimilation is completely contrary to the basic beliefs of their faith. The whole idea of America is unacceptable to a traditional Muslim.

The Murder of Van Gogh

On November 2, 2004, Theo Van Gogh, the great grandson of famous Dutch painter Vincent Van Gogh's brother, was murdered as he rode a bicycle down an Amsterdam street. A twenty-six-year-old man, called Mohammed B. by the police, with dual Dutch and Moroccan nationality, dressed in a traditional Moroccan *jallaba*, fired six shots at Van Gogh (some reports say eight or nine), knocking him to his knees. He then approached his victim who cried out, "Don't do it. Don't do it. Have mercy." With a butcher knife, Mohammed B. sawed into Van Gogh's neck until he nearly severed the head from the body. Using the knife, he then pinned a five-page letter to Van Gogh's chest and calmly walked away.

Theo Van Gogh was a celebrity in Holland. An award-winning filmmaker, television producer and newspaper columnist, he had recently aired a ten-minute film called "Submission." It told the fictional story of a Muslim woman who was forced into an arranged marriage. In the story the veiled woman speaks of being abused by her husband, raped by an uncle and then brutally punished for adultery. In some scenes the actress is dressed in a transparent gown, through which can be seen her body covered with welts and marks from her beatings and various texts from the Qur'an that justify the repression of women.

"Submission" was written by a woman named Ayaan Hirsi Ali. A refugee from Somalia, she fled an arranged marriage, renounced Islam and became an outspoken critic of Muslim customs and of the failure of Muslim immigrants to adapt to Dutch life. Her activism made her popular enough to gain a seat in Parliament.

The film, short as it was, created an outrage among the million Muslims living in Holland. Van Gogh's murder was a direct result of that anger. The letter pinned to his chest was addressed to Hirsi Ali. Ironically, this letter attached to a butchered body began with, "In the name of Allah the kind, the merciful."

What follows are pages of death threats and justifications of violence. A few lines into the letter, the killer wrote, "There is no aggression except against the aggressors," making it clear he believed that Van Gogh and Hirsi Ali were the aggressors because they dared to criticize Islam. Hirsi Ali's weapons were identified as her words.

Since your entrance into the political arena of Holland you have been constantly terrorizing Muslims and Islam with your words. You are not the first and you won't be the last to join the crusade against Islam.

The letter calls her a "soldier of evil" and claims that she had tried to force Muslim children to "make a choice between their creator and the constitution," a reference to her accusations that they were not adapting to Dutch culture. Death appears as the dominant theme of the letter.

Death, Miss Hirsi Ali, is the common theme of all that exists. You, me and the rest of creation can not disconnect from this truth.

Then, in a crescendo of hatred that leads to the conclusion, the letter makes it clear that the aggressive violence of early Islam is alive and well.

Islam will conquer by the blood of the martyrs. It will spread its light to every corner of this Earth and it will, if necessary, drive evil to its dark hole by the sword. This unleashed battle is different from previous battles. The unbelieving fundamentalists have started it and Insha Allah the true believers will end it. There shall be no mercy for the unjust, only the sword raised at them. No discussion, no demonstrations no parades, no petitions; merely DEATH shall separate the Truth from the LIE.

That violent solutions to conflict is a standard of this brand of Islam is indicated by the fact the Mohammed B.

frequently attended the El Tawheed mosque, which, for some time before Van Gogh's murder, had been the subject of heated debate because of a book that they sold telling Muslims to throw homosexuals off the top of tall buildings.

Van Gogh was not exclusively against Muslims either. He was noted for his caustic attacks on just about everyone. He once mocked a prominent Jew and referred to Jesus as "the rotten fish" of Nazareth. None of the Jews or Christians came after him with a butcher knife, however.

We are not saying that all Christians are perfect. There have been many incidents throughout history of Christian violence. (The crusades come to mind.) Neither are we saying that all Muslims are bad people. Most are not.

We are saying, however, that the war against terrorism is a conflict with a large segment of Islam that does not play by the rules of Western culture. While America is always willing to negotiate and to seek a peaceful solution, to the extremists of Islam, peace is not a solution unless it is accomplished by the destruction of their enemies. Even when the attack on Islam is with words, the response is violent. If we have not learned that since the attacks of 9/11, then we are foolish indeed.

There is no safety short of the complete elimination of terrorist ability to function. It is not a matter of leaving them alone and hoping that they will leave us alone. They have proven that they will not. Brute force is the only language that the terrorist can understand.

Terrorism Against the West

Terrorism is the natural product of the religious society of Islamic extremists that are completely opposed to those freedoms that Westerners relish. Terror is probably not quite an accurate name for it, since the goal of terrorists is not simply to kill innocent people. It is rather to destroy the corruption of American ideas so that they will not destroy Islamic tradition. There can be no compromise simply because there is no common ground on which to meet. Van Gogh and Hirsi Ali had to be attacked because their words were a threat to Muslim beliefs.

We have become too familiar with the War on Terror. In fact, Terror has been conducting a war on us for some time. We have been so isolated from it that it had very little impact on us until the tragic attacks of September 11. Now we find ourselves in a struggle for survival.

That struggle emphasizes something that most Americans have ignored for most of our history. The world is now too small for us to remain completely isolated. Our influence on the rest of mankind is no longer a simple byproduct of our success. It is now a necessity for our overall security. If we do not influence the world enough to produce the same regard for individual rights that we enjoy under our Constitution, then we will be constantly attacked by those whose values do not give place to individual rights.

The Great Commission

From a biblical standpoint, we have a responsibility as Christians to attempt to change the thinking of the world. The great commission is exactly that.

> *Go into all the world and preach the gospel*
> *to every creature.* (Mark 16:15)

We recognize that many ungodly things have been done over the centuries in the name of God. The gospel has been used wrongly to justify some of the worst atrocities that have ever been committed. But that does not change the reality that the gospel, proclaimed in a biblical way, establishes the very things that America has claimed as individual rights. The gospel declares God's love for each individual. It validates the worth of the individual. It establishes a belief in an absolute right and wrong and influences society to recognize the value and the rights of others.

If we have a responsibility to influence individuals, then the same can be said for the nation. When the basic unalienable rights upon which American government is founded are expanded to include all people, then the safety of America is insured. As other nations learn to recognize the same rights, they become less likely to infringe on ours. Influencing the world is a necessity for our own safety.

As with any idea or philosophy, freedom cannot be forced on people. They have to be convinced. Military force will not change the thinking of a population. Reason and argument are the only effective means of convincing others. That is why separation of church and state is necessary for religious freedom.

Of course, not everyone wants to listen to the arguments in favor of freedom. Attacks on America are evidence of very different values in other parts of the world. The differences between the world of the West and the world of Islam are the most significant to the safety of America. They are differences that are irreconcilable. It is this fact that makes our influence more important than ever.

Jihads and Fatwas

Great pains have been taken in most Muslim circles to separate the terrorists from the majority of Muslims. Terrorists are painted in terms of a fringe group, a small minority of those who practice Islam, as though terrorism has no basis in true Islamic belief.

Unfortunately, the reality of terrorism does not make such fine distinctions. Terrorism is, for the most part, a religious movement. In D'Souza's words, "the vast majority of Muslims are not terrorists, but it is equally a fact that the vast majority of terrorists are Muslims."[14]

In addition, while most Muslims in the East are not terrorists, they do support the goals and the methods of terrorism. Osama bin Laden became a hero in the Islamic world after the 9/11 attacks. We remember video

★★★★★
Terrorism is,
for the most part,
a religious movement.
★★★★★

broadcasts of thousands in the streets of various Islamic cities cheering at the news of the destruction of the World Trade Center. For more concrete evidence, we have the poll in Gaza that showed 78 percent of Palestinians supported the attacks. Another poll showed that 83 percent of Pakistanis sympathized with bin Laden and al Qaeda.[15] Islamic countries have proven very unwilling to involve themselves in any way in efforts to root out terrorists. While most Muslims are not terrorists, they still applaud the terrorists and think of them as heroes.

A word that has become well-known to Americans over the past few years is *jihad*. It is usually translated by Americans as "holy war." As many Muslim writers are quick to point out, this is not a very accurate rendition. It is more properly "struggle." For the extremists who practice terror, the *jihad* is an open attempt to inflict as much destruction and death on their enemies as possible. More moderate voices have tried to distance themselves from terrorism, at least in a public relations sense, by declaring that the true struggle is an internal one, a struggle against one's self in an effort to follow the path of faithfulness.

This definition, while followed by the vast majority of Muslims in the world, especially those living in the West, is not the definition followed either historically or by the present-day extremists. Historically, *jihad* has been overt and external. Islam has never shied away from violence. To balance that thought, of course, we have to acknowledge that the West has not shied away from violence either. Through much of history, there have been plenty of people and nations ready to attack Islam on religious grounds, usually in the name of Christianity.

But having said that, the general tone of the American public has never been to engage in military conquest. Most of us would like to think that we have grown past the excesses of Christian extremism from the past. Americans really don't like war very much.

But we are faced today with an enemy that does not claim any particular nation as home and whose avowed intent is to destroy our way of life. Even if it is only the extremists that we have to worry about today, there are quite a few of them, and the moderates have proven that they would rather give them refuge than send them away. No matter how we approach the subject, we are dealing with a fanatical religious group who are not interested in discussing our differences.

A look at the passages in the Qur'an that deal with *jihad* can be somewhat sobering to Westerners.

> *So, when the sacred months have passed away, then slay the idolaters wherever you find them, and take them captive and besiege them and lie in wait for them in every ambush, then if they repent, and keep up prayer and pay the poor-rate, leave their way free to them; surely Allah is Forgiving, Merciful.* (Surah 9:5)

That does not sound like a religion of peace that is striving to get along with others and convince them by the quality of Muslim life to convert. Neither does this verse.

> *Fight those who do not believe in Allah, nor in the latter day, nor do they prohibit what Allah and His Apostle have prohibited, nor follow the religion of truth, out of those who have been given the Book, until they pay the tax in acknowledgement of superiority and they are in a state of subjection.* (Surah 9:29)

It is not difficult to see why extremists who are fanatically devoted to Islam feel that the only way to deal with the infidels of the West is to kill them.

> *So when you meet in battle those who disbelieve, then smite the necks until when you have overcome them, then make them prisoners.* (Surah 47:4)

Conversion is accomplished through force.

> *They desire that you should disbelieve as they have disbelieved, so that you might be (all) alike; therefore take not from among them friends until they fly (their homes) in Allah's way; but if they turn back, then seize them and kill them wherever you find them, and take not from among them a friend or a helper.* (Surah 4:89)

This kind of coercion is typical of Islam in past history. This example is from a *fatwa*, a legal judgment or decision by an *ulama* in answer to a question about villages with no mosque.

> *Question: When in several Muslim villages there is not a single mosque, and the inhabitants do not perform the congregational prayers, must the authorities force them to build a mosque and punish those who neglect to pray there?*
> *Answer: Yes. In A.H. 940 [A.D. 1533] express edicts were issued for the attention of the local rulers of the Well-protected [Ottoman] Empire, that they compel the inhabitants of such villages to construct mosques and establish regular prayers. They shall proceed accordingly. Ebu Su'ud wrote as follows, God have mercy on him: "The Call to Prayer is one of the distinguishing characteristics of Islam, so that if the people of a city, town, or village refuse, the Imam should force them, and if they do not do it, he should take up arms against them. And if the people of a town*

neglect the Call to Prayer, the performance of
prayer, and the congregational prayers, he must
fight them, for these are earmarks and outward
signs of religion.[16]

Historically, Muslims sought to expand the frontiers of the faith through military means.[17] For the modern Islamic extremist, the pattern has not changed much. This international form of extremism is the basis for Osama bin Laden's opposition to the United States. The attacks of September 11 were intended to rally Muslims everywhere to a holy war against America. He proclaimed a *jihad* against America and our allies and there is no question that he intended this *jihad* to be something more than an inner struggle to serve God. In a broadcast on October 7, 2001, he described his opinion of the 9/11 attacks. "Allah has blessed a vanguard group of Muslims, the spearhead of Islam, to destroy America."[18]

In the mind of the extremist that we are facing today, destruction of America and the ideals of American life is the entire goal. We have become used to the liberal concept of agreeing to disagree. For the Muslim, the whole idea of allowing your enemy to survive is opposed to the goals of the religion.

The Barbary Pirates

These are hard words for most Americans to swallow. We are supposed to be a moral people, filled with compassion. We cannot bring ourselves to support military action unless we can justify it on moral grounds. We have to be defending ourselves from attack or liberating someone from tyranny before we can condone it. In his farewell address, George

Washington advised his successors to "observe good faith and justice toward all nations." Thomas Jefferson believed in the morality of the nation.

> *It is strangely absurd to suppose that a million of human beings, collected together, are not under the same moral laws which bind each of them separately.*

In keeping with the rights of individuals, it would seem appropriate for a nation to extend the same rights to other nations. If we are to change the minds of other people, it would seem that it must be through persuasion, not through force.

Is there ever a time, then, when the invasion of a country, such as Iraq, is justified? Since we have found precedent in the actions and statements of our Founding Fathers for so many other situations, is there such a precedent for invasion?

In fact, most Americans would probably be surprised at the number of times United States armed forces have been committed to actions in other countries. It totals more than two hundred and thirty. The earliest were between 1798 and 1800 during an undeclared war with France. American troops were landed in the city of Puerto Plata in the Dominican Republic where marines captured a French privateer. The most memorable actions, however, came during the presidency of Thomas Jefferson and involved a long and bitter confrontation with Islam. Confrontations between the United States and Islam are not new.

The first great test of American foreign policy came from four Muslim states along the coast of northern Africa

– Morocco, Algiers, Tunis and Tripoli. Known to Americans as the Barbary Pirates, these nations practiced a kind of protection racket on an international scale. Piracy was a national industry.

The pattern was simple. A Barbary Coast ruler declared war on a foreign nation whose trade regularly passed through the Mediterranean. Ships from the pirate nation, licensed as warships, then sailed to capture enemy vessels. The prizes were hauled into their harbors. Ships and cargo were sold for whatever could be gotten. In every city of North Africa, there were regular slave auctions in which the "Christian" captives were sold. The stronger men were put to work on public projects. The better-looking women were sold as concubines. Occasionally young boys were sold to rich pederasts. If the prices for the slave market were down, the captives were thrown into a dungeon until the market improved.[19] Hostage taking and impossible demands from Islamic radicals are not new either.

The British devised a method of dealing with this threat. They simply paid tribute so that the Barbary nations would leave their shipping alone. They found that an adroit use of that tribute also meant that the pirates would attack everyone else's ships and thereby limit competition for British merchants. These nonaggression pacts became a standard part of Britain's Mediterranean policy.[20]

Of course, other nations were quick to join in. By the time of the American Revolution, nearly every country that had ships in the Mediterranean was paying tribute. As long as they were colonies of Great Britain, the American merchants enjoyed the protection of British tribute. After the Revolution, however, things changed.

The first incident was the capture of the merchant brig *Betsey* by Morocco in October, 1784. This was an odd act of piracy. However, it did demonstrate the whimsical nature of Barbary politics. The ruler of Morocco, Emperor Mawlay Muhammad, was the second, after France, to recognize American independence. Since 1778, he had been waiting for the Americans to send a negotiator. He claimed that he wanted to develop commercial treaties with the Americans and promised protection for their ships. Since America had failed to send any representatives, he decided to get their attention. The *Betsey* and her crew were to be held until America sent an ambassador.[21]

There followed more serious actions, however. Algiers was a much more formidable and dangerous opponent. Algerian corsairs captured the American schooner *Maria* just a few months after the *Betsey* incident. A week later, the *Dauphin* was taken off Cadiz.

The stories told later by some of the captives horrified Americans. James Leander Cathcart was one of six crewmen on the *Maria*. He later released a first-hand account of his experience. Algerian seamen swarmed aboard and forced the crew to strip to their underwear. They were herded on board the Algerian xebec and forced below deck, crammed in with thirty-six men and a woman from other prizes.[22] Upon arrival in Algiers, they were kept for three days in prison, then auctioned off at the slave market.[23] Cathcart related many instances of cruelty to the prisoners. They were beaten regularly and put to hard labor in the most unsanitary and cruel conditions. Their captors seemed to take a sadistic pleasure in the torture. On one occasion, Cathcart described how a Genoese man had actually been ransomed by his native country and was being released.

*. . . a Genoese on his redemption, kissing the
hand of Mahomed Bashaw, Dey of Algiers,
inadvertently said, "thank God I have been your
servant ten years and never received the
bastinado once." "Did you not," said the Dey?
"Take this Christian and give him one hundred
blows on the soles of his feet, that he may not have
so great a miracle to tell his countrymen when he
returns to his home." The poor man, thunder
struck, exclaimed "I am free! Surely your
Excellency will not punish me for not having
committed a fault in ten years' captivity?" "Give
him two hundred blows," replied the Dey, "and if
the Infidel says a word more, send him to the works
again and inform the person, that has redeemed
him, that he may have anyone of the same nation
in his room. I will keep him till he dies, for his
insolence."*[24]

Cathcart spent eleven years in captivity. He would later
become the U.S. consul general to the Barbary States.[25]

The brig *Polly* was bound for Cadiz when it was
captured by the Algerian vessel *Babazera*. John Foss, one
of the crew, later told his story of their captivity. They were
stripped to their shirts and undershorts, taken aboard the
Algerian corsair and brought to the captain's cabin.[26] Rais
Hudga Mahomet Salamia, the captain, ordered them to help
man his brig. One of the crew protested that they could not
work a ship in their underwear, since the pirate crew had taken
everything else.

He answered in very abusive words, that we might think ourselves well used that they did not take them. And he would teach us to work naked, adding "now you are slaves and must be treated as such, and do not think that you will be treated worse than you really deserve, for your bigotry and superstition, in believing in a man who was crucified by the Jews, and disregarding the true doctrine of God's last and greatest prophet, Mahomet." He then ordered us immediately to our duty.[27]

Foss reported that the prisoners were taken into the port of Algiers and marched through the streets. Mobs lined the way, shouting and clapping joyously, thanking God for "their great success, and victories over so many Christian dogs, and unbelievers, which is the appellation they generally give to all christians."[28]

They were put to work in a rock quarry, cutting and carrying boulders that weighed many tons. They were regularly beaten for the most trivial offenses.

They are continually beating the slaves with their sticks, and goading them with its end, in which is a small spear, not unlike an ox goad, among our farmers. If anyone chance to faint, and fall down with fatigue, they generally beat them until they are able to rise again.[29]

Bastinadoes were a common punishment. Men's legs were tied to a pole and raised off the ground. Guards then struck the soles of their feet with clubs. For capital offenses, some prisoners were burned or roasted alive. Others were impaled on sharp iron stakes. A slave found with a Muslim woman was beheaded. The mere suspicion of being with a woman resulted in castration. Killing another slave was punished with beheading. Slaves who killed a Muslim were thrown off walls that had iron hooks about half way down. Often men would hang there for days before dying.[30]

On one occasion, fourteen slaves escaped in a small boat. They were overtaken and the ringleaders beheaded. The rest received 500 bastinadoes each and then had a fifty-pound weights attached to their legs for life.[31] The crime of disparaging the Qur'an was punished with roasting alive, impalement or crucifixion.[32]

Thirty-five American ships and a total of about 700 sailors were captured by the Barbary States between 1785 and 1815.[33] Many of the prisoners died in captivity. Others were held for as long as twelve years. As stories of the Muslim brutality spread through America, so did hatred of Muslims.

Algiers declared war on the United States in July of 1785. In November, two men and a woman arrived in Virginia from North Africa. Patrick Henry was the governor at the time and all kinds of rumors were circulating about spies from Algiers.[34] Henry ordered the strangers to be locked up in Norfolk, then Williamsburg and finally Richmond. They were interrogated at some length. In their luggage there was a small amount of cash, some documents in Hebrew and some English traveling papers. They said the documents were to admit them into a temple. The questioners could not read Hebrew so there was no way to verify the claim. The prisoners said they were from England, but the papers suggested Morocco.[35]

Eventually, these innocent Jewish pilgrims were sent back to Morocco and the Virginia legislature quickly passed deportation laws to insure that such dangerous aliens would never bother good Americans again.[36]   Racial profiling is another thing that is not new.

The Shores of Tripoli

Most Americans preferred paying the tribute to engaging in war.[37]   Thomas Jefferson was acting as the U.S. ambassador to France at the time and it fell to him to try to arrange negotiations. He quickly figured out that negotiation would not accomplish much. He realized that the tribute that was being demanded was far more than the American government could afford and that paying it would only result in the demand for more. His recommendation was military action.

Congress saw it otherwise, however, and they voted to pay the tribute. It amounted to almost one-sixth of the entire federal budget at the time. Ultimately, the tribute brought the release of the 119 Americans being held at that time in Algiers. But then Tripoli demanded a similar treaty. Not long after, Algiers demanded more as well. Jefferson was proved correct.

The United States Navy began as a direct response to the conflict with Algiers. Congress narrowly voted to construct six frigates, beginning in March of 1794. The construction resulted in ships that later became famous during the War of 1812, such as the *Constitution* and the *United States*. When Jefferson became president, he had this naval force at his disposal.

Five days after his inauguration, Jefferson met with his Cabinet to discuss the situation with the Barbary States. The discussion was not so much about the need to send ships to the Mediterranean to protect American shipping as it was over the requirements of the Constitution regarding the use of military force. No American vessels could attack another nation without a declaration of war from Congress.[38] The manner in which Jefferson proceeded said a great deal about how he viewed the limits of the Constitution. Of all the Founding Fathers, he was probably the most opposed to a strong central government, the most against a standing army and certainly the most inclined to do nothing without the consent of the Congress. He was a strict constitutionalist.

> The manner in which Jefferson proceeded said a great deal about how he viewed the limits of the Constitution.

It was agreed that a squadron could be sent to the Mediterranean, as long as it merely guarded American merchantmen from attack. Four days later, the Cabinet received word from Tripoli that cruisers there were being fitted out to attack American ships.[39]

Jefferson made the decision to send warships. Congress was in recess, but he did not call for a special session. Secretary of the Navy, General Samuel Smith, issued orders for the squadron to attack only if attacked, to protect American shipping and to defend any American vessel against attack. The orders also stated that, if the commodore of the squadron discovered that any of the Barbary States had declared war on the United States, regardless of the fact that Congress had not issued a declaration of war, he was authorized to "chastise their insolence by sinking, burning or destroying their ships and vessels wherever you shall find them."[40] If Tripoli declared war, the Americans were to blockade that port and allow no vessels in or out.

Jefferson did not call a special session of Congress even when he received word that Tripoli had declared war. He waited until they were in regular session and then asked for the declaration. There was considerable debate with arguments familiar to modern Americans. Congressmen were concerned about the cost and the fact that we had no allies in Europe. In fact, Britain and France were both hostile to intervention. They preferred to keep the Americans out of the Mediterranean altogether. French hostility is certainly not new. Others were worried that a military action would put the hostages into even greater danger, a position that infuriated many of the hostages.

When it was over, however, Congress knew that something had to be done. They decided not to declare war but rather to give a specific statutory authorization, a practice that has been considered constitutional from the very beginning. It is worth noting that the Constitution does not require a declaration of war for a president to engage in military action. It requires the "Advise and Consent of the Senate." For Jefferson, this came in the form of the February 6, 1802 "Act to Authorize the Defense of the Merchant Vessels of the United States against French Depredations." The scope of the act included other nations than France.

> *Be it enacted by the Senate and House of Representatives of the United States of America in Congress Assembled, that it shall be lawful fully to equip, officer, man, and employ such of the*

> *armed vessels of the United States as may be judged requisite by the President of the United States, for protecting effectually the commerce and seamen thereof on the Atlantic ocean, the Mediterranean and adjoining seas.*

In fact, there was not much limitation put on the President's discretionary powers.

> *And be it further enacted, That it shall be lawful for the President of the United States to instruct the commanders of the respective public vessels aforesaid, to subdue, seize and make prize of all vessels, goods and effects, belonging to the Bey of Tripoli, or to his subjects, and to bring or send the same into port, to be proceeded against, and distributed according to law; and also to cause to be done all such other acts of precaution or hostility as the state of war will justify, and may, in his opinion, require.*

Ultimately, what President Jefferson felt was required was a full-scale attack on Tripoli combined with a land assault from Egypt. The naval actions produced some of America's earliest heroes and the land action has been immortalized in the Marine anthem with the line "to the shores of Tripoli." It is true that there were only eight marines and a midshipman in the force, but they served with great distinction and contributed early to the proud heritage of the U.S. Marine Corps. The rest of the land force was a multinational collection from twelve countries. Coalitions against Islamic nations are also not new.

Ultimately, the Bey of Tripoli was forced into a treaty under which he left American trade alone. It established a precedent that astonished the rest of the world. None of the Barbary States were willing to go to war with the United States after that. Jefferson achieved peace on his own terms. It was not entirely the end of the conflict. There were still occasional incidents, but nothing like what had been happening. And America was the only nation not paying tribute.

[1]We appreciate Phil Cooke taking the time to relate this story in a phone interview.

[2]D'Souza, *What's So Great About America*, pg. 41-42.

[3]Lee, *The Producer's Business Handbook*, pg. 34.

[4]Phil Cooke interview.

[5]Ralston, *Importing the European Army*, pg. 1.

[6]D'Souza, *What's So Great About America*, pg. 62-63.

[7]*Ibid.*, pg. 77.

[8]*Ibid.*, pg. 16.

[9]*Ibid.*, pg. 17.

[10]*Ibid.*, pg. 21.

[11]Kepel, *Jihad*, pg. 5.

[12]*Ibid.*, pg. 9.

[13]Ramadon, *Western Muslims and The Future of Islam*, pg. 4.

[14]D'Souza, *What's So Great About America*, pg. 9.

[15]*Ibid.*

[16]*Ibid.*, pg. 133.

[17]Ralston, *Importing the European Army*, pg. 48.

[18]Kepel, *Jihad*, pg. 2.

[19]Whipple, *To the Shores of Tripoli*, pg. 20-21.

[20]*Ibid.*, pg. 21.

[21]Allison, *The Crescent Obscured*, pg. 110-111.

[22]Baepler, *White Slaves, African Masters*, pg. 107-108.

[23]Whipple, *To the Shores of Tripoli*, pg. 26.

[24]Baepler, *White Slaves, African Masters*, pg. 114.

[25]*Ibid.*, pg. 103.

[26]*Ibid.*, pg. 75-76)

[27]Foss, *A Journal, of the Captivity and Sufferings of John Foss*, pg. 11.

[28]Baepler, *White Slaves, African Masters*, pg. 78.

[29]*Ibid.*, pg. 81.

[30]*Ibid.*, pg. 83.

[31]*Ibid.*

[32]Whipple, *To the Shores of Tripoli*, pg. 40.

[33]Allison, *The Crescent Obscured*, pg. 110.

[34]*Ibid.*, pg. 3.

[35]*Ibid.*, pg. 5-6.

[36]*Ibid.*, pg. 6.

[37]*Ibid.*, pg. 7.

[38]Whipple, *To the Shores of Tripoli*, pg. 64.

[39]*Ibid.*

[40]*Ibid.*, pg. 66.

★★★★★

Individual Right #12

The Right To Be Informed

★★★★★

Responsibility #12

Know The Truth

★★★★★

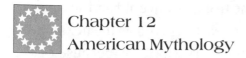

Chapter 12
American Mythology

> *I am not bound to win, but I am bound to be true. I am not bound to succeed, but I am bound to live by the light that I have. I must stand with anybody that stands right, stand with him while he is right, and part with him when he goes wrong.*
> (Abraham Lincoln)

Americans have developed a kind of mythology over the past two centuries. There are many things that we have learned from childhood that make very patriotic stories, but which actually aren't true. Many of these myths are harmless, such as the story of Washington chopping down the cherry tree or throwing a silver dollar across the Potomac. (The original stories had him barking a cherry tree and throwing a stone across the Rappahanock. But even those stories are fiction.) Others have more significance.

If asked to pick the one person who most contributed to the American victory in the Revolutionary War, most would name someone like George Washington. There was one person who is not as well known, however, who may have saved the entire war almost single-handedly. His contributions are almost unknown to most Americans and his story indicates the degree to which we have believed legends and myths of American history that are just not true.

It was the winter of 1777-1778. Washington's Continental Army was in camp at Valley Forge, infamous for the hardships endured by the troops from cold and starvation. The truth was that it was not nearly as cold as the next winter proved to be and most of the starvation was because of the inept way that the American government procured supplies. There was plenty of food available but the local farmers preferred to sell to the British in Philadelphia. American money was almost worthless. The British were happily waiting out the winter, warm and cozy, while the Americans suffered.

In February, a sleigh arrived at camp with a forty-seven-year-old Prussian officer accompanied by an Italian greyhound and followed by a carriage, five grooms and drivers, a military secretary, two French aides and three servants. It was Friedrich Wilhelm Ludolf Gerhard Augustin, Baron von Steuben.[1] He came with a letter from Benjamin Franklin and Silas Deane, the American ambassadors in Paris at the time, introducing him as a lieutenant general who had served under Frederick the Great of Prussia and recommending him to Washington's service.[2]

In actual fact, he had only been a captain and his service with the Prussian army ended with the Seven Years War.[3] But Steuben brought something to the Americans that was desperately needed – drill. And he proved to be so effective that even when Washington discovered the lies, he decided to overlook them.

Steuben put together a company of one hundred men and began working with them as though he was a drill sergeant. He taught them the most basic elements of marching in various formations, how to deploy from column into line, how to load and fire their muskets effectively and how to use the bayonet.

As he worked with his model company, Steuben created a simplified version of the Prussian drill manual. He didn't speak a word of English, so it had to be written in French and translated to English. As the work continued, it eventually became the *Regulations for the Order and Discipline of the Troops of the United States*. This manual continued in use by the American army all the way up to the War of 1812.

The drill attracted much attention around the camp and, as the system developed, more men were included until the whole army was training every day. Much of it was comical. Since he didn't know English, Steuben had to give orders through a couple of aides who acted as translators. He tried to learn a few phrases, but it was slow work. At times he would burst into a rage and swear profusely, though in Prussian, which more often caused amusement to the troops than fear. One of his aides, Duponceau, recalled some of the episodes.

> *When some movement or maneuver was not performed to his mind he began to swear in German, then in French, and then in both languages together. When he had exhausted his artillery of foreign oaths, he would call to his aides, "My dear Walker and my dear Duponceau, come and swear for me in English. These fellows won't do what I bid them."*[4]

The Myth of the Citizen Soldier

It is a long-held belief by most Americans that we won the war because American soldiers wore blue and hid behind trees while the British wore red and marched in straight lines. Nothing could be further from the truth. The weapons of the day dictated that battles be fought exactly in the way that they were.

The primary weapon was the smoothbore, muzzle-loading, flintlock musket. The standard British issue was the Short Land Service Musket or the "Brown Bess," as it was commonly known. It had a barrel thirty-nine inches long and it weighed about eleven pounds.[5] The Americans used a collection of older weapons but they all worked basically the same.

Loading and firing was a complicated process that took some time and training to master. The bullet had to be rammed down the barrel of the musket, which meant that it had to be slightly smaller than the barrel itself. As a result, accuracy was limited. Rifles were more accurate because the rifling inside the barrel made the bullet spin as it came out and caused its flight to be straighter and more consistent. The drawback was that in order to make the bullet fit tight enough for the rifling to work, it became difficult to get the bullet into the barrel. You almost had to hammer it down. A rifle took three to four times as long to load as a musket, a great drawback in the heat of battle.

★★★★★

Speed was almost always preferred in combat to accuracy.

★★★★★

Speed was almost always preferred in combat to accuracy. Most military muskets didn't even have a rear sight. It was expected that the soldier would simply point in the general direction of the enemy and pull the trigger. This meant that very few bullets ever actually hit anything. The comments of Major George Hanger, a military authority of the time, give some idea of the range of muskets.

> *A soldier's musket, if not exceedingly ill bored (as many of them are) will strike . . . a man at eighty yards; it may even at 100. But a soldier must be very unfortunate indeed who shall be wounded by a common musket at 150 yards; and as to firing at a man at two hundred yards, you might as well fire at the moon.*[6]

Added to the relative difficulty of hitting a target was the fact that the firing mechanism was remarkably unreliable. As many as 15 percent of the muskets failed to fire during dry conditions. If it was wet, it could go as high as 25 percent.[7]

During a battle, things got even worse. After the first volley, the smoke from the guns would hang in the air so thick that it was very likely the soldier would not even be able to see his enemy through most of the firefight. In all of the confusion, most troops were lucky to get off much more than one shot a minute.

These factors dictated the kinds of formations that were used on the battlefield. If you did not cram as many men as possible into as small an area as possible, there was no hope of hitting anything. The drill manual that the British used during the American Revolution specified that a line would consist of two ranks of men, standing elbow to elbow.[8] Twenty-two inches were allotted to each file. The front rank knelt while the back rank stood. Other nationalities used three ranks.[9]

Even with that kind of a target, most firefights took place at twenty to eighty yards, less than the distance of a

football field. The average seems to be around seventy-five.[10]
Even with that kind of a target, the muskets still hit remarkably
few of the enemy. A variety of experts give percentages that
range from as low as .03 percent to 5 percent. Most put
effectiveness at less than one percent.[11] Marshal Saxe, a
prominent French general of the period, stated in his memoirs,
"I have seen whole volleys fired, without even killing four
men."[12] Examples from European combat, such as the attack
of Major General von Sporcke's column at the battle of
Minden, show about 2 percent effectiveness on average.[13]

There are many examples during the American Revolution
that show how ineffective musket fire really was. At the Concord
Bridge, a British company fired at over one hundred Americans
at less than fifty yards range. They hit two.[14] During the retreat
back to Boston, the British suffered 273 casualties out of the
1,800 men involved. The 3,763 American colonists involved were
considered to be pretty good shots. They fired approximately
75,000 times during the course of the day. That means that only
one shot in 300 actually hit the British, even though they were
wearing red and marching in straight lines.[15] Thomas Jefferson,
in a letter reporting the casualties from Lexington and Concord,
attributed the British casualties to American accuracy.

*This difference is ascribed to our superiority
in taking aim when we fire; every soldier in our
army having been intimate with his gun from his
infancy.*

This should give a better idea of why it was so important
that Baron von Steuben trained the Americans to march in
straight lines the same way the British did. It was impossible

to stand up to the disciplined professionalism of the British army without that training. It is easy to forget that the Americans had a pretty bad losing streak going before Valley Forge. As much as we like to remember Bunker Hill as a great moment in our history, the fact is that the British won the battle. They also won at Long Island, Kip's Bay, Harlem Heights, White Plains, Fort Washington, and Fort Lee. The idea of the militia army

The idea of the militia army standing up to the British is a myth.

standing up to the British is a myth. It did not happen. It was the training at Valley Forge that gave the American troops the competence to wage war effectively.

The first action of the spring after Valley Forge was at Monmouth. At one point during the action, Americans were retreating and Washington brought up fresh troops to reorganize the position. In the confusion, the newly-trained soldiers reacted with great calm, marching to their places without any sign of panic. Steuben appeared in the middle of the maneuvers, shouting out the commands that he had been using all winter. Captain Alexander Hamilton expressed the feelings of most of the officers when he said that he had never appreciated the value of military discipline until that moment.[16]

This is just one of the myths of American history, the belief that an amateur army can defend a nation against a well-trained professional force. It is a myth that dies hard. Yet there are reasons to cling to the concept of a citizen army. Personal freedom has always been connected to the idea of defending hearth and home.

A Well-Regulated Militia

America is founded more than anything else on the idea that each individual has certain rights that are not dependent on government. No matter how many people might vote for something, they cannot remove those rights without violating the will of God. America was also founded on the understanding that the individual has every right to defend those rights against any aggressor. When Benjamin Franklin came out of the Constitutional Convention, a woman asked him what kind of government they had given to America. He answered, "A republic, madam, if you can keep it." He was also the one who was careful to differentiate between a simple democracy in which the majority rules and a republic in which the individual is protected from the majority.

> *Democracy is two wolves and a lamb voting on what to have for lunch. Liberty is a well-armed lamb contesting the vote.* (Benjamin Franklin)

Democracy was not something spoken of favorably by any of the Founding Fathers. They equated it with anarchy. Roger Sherman, the delegate from Connecticut, speaking at the Convention, said that people "should have as little to do as may be about the government. They want information and are constantly liable to be misled."[17] Elbridge Gerry, undoubtedly referring to Shay's Rebellion, which had only recently been subdued in western Massachusetts, claimed, "The evils we experience flow from the excess of democracy."[18]

The Second Amendment is one of the results of that understanding that the lamb needs to be well-armed in a free society. Its precise meaning has been hotly debated in recent decades but the original intent is not difficult to discern in the context of early America.

> *A well regulated Militia, being necessary to the security of a free State, the right of the people to keep and bear Arms, shall not be infringed.* (Second Amendment)

The debate is over just what is meant by the term "militia." Some are sure that the right to bear arms belongs only to the militia. Others are sure that the right to bear arms belongs to the individuals who make up the militia.

We must look at a little of the background of this Amendment. It was a concept that the Founding Fathers had instilled in them as one of the rights of Englishmen that they felt was being taken away from them. Blackstone spoke of it as a part of English heritage and there was no ambiguity about what he thought it meant. In his *Commentaries*, he referred to the three primary rights of Englishmen – personal security, personal liberty, and private property. He then said there were five auxiliary rights that served to protect the primary ones. It is the fifth of those auxiliary rights that we are concerned with here.

> *The fifth and last auxiliary right of the subject, that I shall at present mention, is that of having arms for their defence suitable to their condition and degree, and such as are allowed by law . . . and it is indeed a public allowance under due restrictions, of the natural right of resistance and self preservation, when the sanctions of society*

and laws are found insufficient to restrain the violence of oppression.

The right to bear arms was necessary for self-preservation when society and law failed to protect the individual. This was not new to Blackstone either. He got it from a nearly two hundred-year-old heritage extending back to the time of the English Civil War.

As far back as the time of the Norman conquest, the British did not think of the possession of weapons as an individual right. It was an individual duty, an unpopular duty, that the government imposed.[19] Every able-bodied man between the ages of sixteen and sixty was required to own a weapon so that he could serve in the militia which could be called out at any time for the defense of the nation or to help deal with crime, since there was no police department. Gun control laws were not designed to keep British citizens from owning guns. They were intended to require ownership.

The idea of having arms for personal protection was deeply entrenched in English thinking.

The individual ownership was always a factor. In 1569, for example, Queen Elizabeth's Privy Council thought it would be a good idea to have the government store militia weapons at a central location. There was such overwhelming opposition that the idea was dropped immediately.[20]

It was during the reign of James I and Charles I that the Crown moved toward keeping a standing army during peacetime instead of relying on a militia army. During the First Bishops' War, Charles discovered that a militia army that didn't agree with the war is remarkably unreliable and he wanted a military force more closely under his control.[21]

Charles didn't restrict weapon ownership but he did try to create a government monopoly over ammunition.[22] By the end of the English Civil War, Parliament was in a position to force concessions and he gave up the monopoly.[23] Further conflict eventually led to the execution of Charles I on January 30, 1649 and the rule of Parliament without a king.

Parliament attempted some restrictions on weapons, primarily aimed at their opponents, but the general population grew increasingly hostile toward government infringements. When Oliver Cromwell, the driving force behind the government, died in 1658, there was such turmoil in the country that the exiled son of the executed king, Charles II, was invited to return to England and reestablish the monarchy.

The years of civil war emphasized the precarious position of the king of England. Parliament put him on the throne and Parliament could remove him. To secure his position, Charles implemented a number of measures designed to maintain a standing army he could rely on at the same time that access to arms by the militia was restricted. In December, 1660, gunsmiths were ordered to provide a list of all the weapons they had made for the past six months and who had purchased them. They were also ordered to report their sales every week so that the government could keep track of just who had guns.[24] Houses were searched and arms confiscated from anyone considered a threat to the Crown.

The idea of having arms for personal protection was deeply entrenched in English thinking, however, and the attempts by the government to confiscate guns were met with such a public outrage that generally the Crown troops had to back off and apologize.[25] Juries rarely voted to convict anyone put on trial for having illegal weapons.

In spite of the laws, actual court records show quite a bit of leniency in the way people were treated. The general view of everyone was that firearms were a necessary part of self-defense. Attempts at controlling them were consistently resisted.[26]

After Charles died in 1685, his brother came to the throne as King James II. James steadily tried to build up a standing army loyal to him and made even greater efforts to limit the militia than Charles had done. He was outspokenly Catholic. He took steps to replace Protestant officers with loyal Catholics, intending to turn all of England into a Catholic nation. These changes were extremely unpopular in a basically Protestant nation.

Matters reached a point of crisis when disaffected Protestants invited William of Orange, James' son-in-law, to come to England and restore liberty.[27] James was forced to flee to the continent when virtually the entire army deserted to join William, and the militia refused to serve.

The Declaration of Rights

Parliament was not anxious to hand over power again without some guarantees. Two kings in a row had tried to restrict what Englishmen considered basic liberties, and before they declared William to be king, they wanted a few things cleared up. The two principal issues were the creation of a standing army and the disarming of the militia.[28]

In January, 1689, the House of Commons began debate on the rights of Englishmen. It was determined that a committee should draft a document that asserted the "Rights and Liberties of the Nation."[29] The resulting "Declaration of Rights" listed thirteen rights and liberties that were considered as "true, ancient, and indubitable."[30]

The issue of arms was a significant part of the discussion. Sir John Maynard, the oldest man in the House at the age of eighty-six, declared it "an abominable thing to disarm a nation."[31] To the objection that a fully armed populace would enable many to destroy game in violation of hunting laws, Thomas Erle made a statement that might be the predecessor of the modern saying, "Guns don't kill people, people kill people."

> *There is a law made against it soe that tis not the gun or musket that offends but the man that makes an ill use of his Armes and he may be punished for it by the law.*[32]

Article 6 of the Declaration dealt with the right to bear arms. The original version that came out of the committee read:

> *That the subjects, which are Protestants, may provide and keep Arms, for their common Defense.*

When the bill was discussed by both the House of Commons and the House of Lords, the wording was changed slightly.

> *That the Subjects which are Protestants may have Arms for their Defence suitable to their Conditions and as allowed by Law.*

There are two things significant about this article. First of all, prior to this, the bearing of arms was considered to be an obligation. From this time forward, it was declared to be a right. The article read "may have arms," not "must have arms."

The second thing is the shift in emphasis when the article was changed. "Common defense" became "their defense." What could have been a right given to the militia only became a right given to the individual. Joyce Lee Malcolm, in *To Keep and Bear Arms*, describes the shift in emphasis.

> *On the other hand, although downplaying the role of the armed citizenry in maintaining liberty, the article claimed for the individual a right to be armed. In light of this shift, it is particularly ironic that some modern American lawyers have misread the English right to have arms as merely a "collective" right inextricably tied to the need for a militia. In actual fact, the Convention retreated steadily from such a position and finally came down squarely, and exclusively, in favour of an individual right to have arms for self-defence. Not only was the militia left out of the Declaration of Rights, but even the notion that private arms were necessary for common, as opposed to individual, defence was excluded.*

The emphasis on the individual right can be seen also in the way Catholics were treated. In spite of the nearly universal fear that Catholics would rise up in rebellion, it was still believed that they should have arms for self-defense. John Maynard recommended ". . . that all those of that religion bring all their fire-arms in, unless for the necessary defence of their Houses, to officers appointed."[33]

As standing armies became more common, they began to take over the duties of police, and the militia became less important. The right to bear arms became almost entirely focused on individual self-defense in the thinking of all Englishmen.

There is no doubt that the individual ownership of guns is what was intended by the Declaration of Rights. In 1780, there were some riots in London. The Recorder of London was asked if the right to arms protected armed groups. He answered:

> *The right of his majesty's Protestant subjects, to have arms for their own defence, and to use them for lawful purposes, is most clear and undeniable. It seems, indeed, to be considered, by the ancient laws of this kingdom, not only as a right, but as a duty; for all the subjects of the realm, who are able to bear arms, are bound to be ready, at all times, to assist the sheriff, and other civil magistrates, in the execution of the laws and the preservation of the public peace. And that right, which every Protestant most unquestionably possesses, individually, may, and in many cases must, be exercised collectively, is likewise a point*

which I conceive to be most clearly established by the authority of judicial decisions and ancient acts of parliament, as well as by reason and common sense.[34]

The Second Amendment

When the new United States created the Bill of Rights, the Second Amendment was intended to accomplish two things. It was intended first of all to provide for the defense of the nation without allowing a standing army to gain too much power. But it also followed the tradition of the English Bill of Rights in guaranteeing the individual's right to have weapons for self-defense.

Most of the various State Constitutions made it clear that they intended the right to bear arms to refer to individuals. Militia acts nearly always contained such phrases as in the Virginia Bill of Rights, "a well-regulated Militia, composed of the body of the people, trained to arms, is the proper, natural, and safe defence of a free State." A distinction was made between the general militia, which consisted of all the people, and a select militia that was specially trained, such as our modern National Guard. It was the people who were to be armed. For example, John Smiley, a member of the Pennsylvania convention, expressed his concerns over a standing army. "When a select militia is

★★★★★

A distinction was made between the general militia, which consisted of all the people, and a select militia.

★★★★★

formed, the people in general may be disarmed."[35] Theodore Sedgwick of Massachusetts doubted that a nation like America could ever be enslaved, as long as the people remained armed. "Is it possible . . . that an army could be raised for the purpose of enslaving themselves or their brethren? or, if raised whether they could subdue a nation of freemen, who know how to prize liberty and who have arms in their hands?"

Congress established control over militia of the various states in the Militia Act of 1792. Among other things, that act specified that the militia was to be made up of every free able-bodied white male citizen between eighteen and forty-five years of age. It also specified that they were required to have their own weapons.

> *That every citizen, so enrolled and notified, shall, within six months thereafter, provide himself with a good musket or firelock, a sufficient bayonet and belt, two spare flints, and a knapsack, a pouch, with a box therein, to contain not less than twenty four cartridges, suited to the bore of his musket or firelock, each cartridge to contain a proper quantity of power and ball.*

When America started, there was no distinction between militia and the people. George Mason, a delegate at the Constitutional Convention, made it clear.

> *I ask, Who are the militia? They consist now of the whole people.*

Richard Henry Lee wrote that America needed to guard against a "select militia," by encouraging a "general militia."

> *All regulations tending to render this general militia useless and defenceless, by establishing select corps of militia, or distinct bodies of military men, not having permanent interests and attachments in the community to be avoided.*

In 1903, that was precisely what happened. The state militias were transformed into units of the National Guard with the passage of the Dick Act. By 1911, they were organized into standard units of infantry, field artillery, coast artillery, cavalry, engineers and signal. The National Defense Act of 1916 specifically designated the National Guard as the Army's primary reserve, and the state militias came to an end.

But that change in no way alters the original intention that the individual citizen be guaranteed the right to bear arms for his own defense. The Founding Fathers never intended that the militia be construed as a state organization. They were always thinking of the rights of the individual citizen to keep arms, in exactly the manner of their heritage from the English Bill of Rights. What America did was to remove the restrictions. Instead of being just for Protestants, the right to bear arms extended to all citizens.

It does not require much reading to find comments that make the thinking of early American leaders clear.

> *And that the said Constitution be never construed to authorize Congress to infringe the*

just liberty of the Press, or the rights of Conscience; or to prevent the people of the Untied States, who are peaceable citizens, from keeping their own arm. . . . (Samuel Adams)

The constitutions of most of our States assert that all power is inherent in the people; that . . . it is their right and duty to be at all times armed. . . (Thomas Jefferson)

No Free man shall ever be debarred the use of arms. (Thomas Jefferson)

A free people ought not only to be armed . . . (George Washington)

The primary reason given by all of the Founding Fathers for keeping the people armed is to act as a check on tyrannical government.

To disarm the people [is] the best and most effectual way to enslave them. (George Mason)

Noah Webster identified the right to bear arms with the safety of the nation.

Before a standing army can rule, the people must be disarmed; as they are in almost every kingdom of Europe. The supreme power in America cannot enforce unjust laws by the sword; because the whole body of the people are armed, and constitute a force superior to any bands of regular troops. (Noah Webster)

James Madison claimed that this was the greatest difference between the United States and other nations.

Besides the advantage of being armed, which the Americans possess over the people of almost every other nation, . . . in the several kingdoms of Europe, . . . the governments are afraid to trust the people with arms. (James Madison)

In the eyes of those who wrote the Constitution, the right to bear arms was an individual right, not a militia right. The Senators who approved the original Bill of Rights, purposely deleted the phrase "for the common defense" after "to keep and bear arms." They did it for the same reason that the English Parliament decided not to use the same words. They never intended the right to be for a militia. It was for the general militia which was made up of the individual citizens. They would never have considered the National Guard to be the general militia. The defense of the country should always rest with the people themselves.

The Danger of Disarming

Things have changed over the past two hundred years, of course. The questions asked by those who want to see firearms eliminated are valid. The general belief is that banning guns would prevent violent crimes. Is a gun really necessary for self-defense in the average life of ordinary citizens? Wouldn't we be better off to curb violence by removing the instruments of violence?

First of all, the degree to which guns are used in self-defense might surprise you. A national survey in 1993 by Gary Kleck, a criminologist at Florida State University, showed that there are approximately 2 million defensive gun uses every year by law-abiding citizens. Another study by the Department of Justice in 1994 estimated 1.5 million uses of guns in self-defense. It does happen quite often in America.

We also have statistics available from places that have banned guns. If the critics are right, then we should see drops in violent crime in those places. The reasons for passing those laws were invariably attached to some violent crime incident in the first place and the desire of the people to prevent such things from happening again.

In 1996, for example, a madman went on a killing spree that ended the lives of sixteen children and a teacher in Dunblane, Scotland. Britain's gun control laws were already tight, but after that, guns were virtually eliminated. Citizens turned in 162,000 registered weapons to the police.

Over the next two years, however, the criminal use of handguns increased 40 percent. Robberies increased 81 percent in England and Wales. Vehicle theft increased 53 percent. The clear violation of the right to self-protection became blatant when a 93-year-old woman in England put up barbed wire around her home after repeated burglaries. The BBC reported in August, 2001 that the government ordered her to remove it because it could injure intruders. One gets the impression that we are trying to protect the criminals.

Canada began to ban handguns in 1930, so there has been a long history of gun control there. By stages, other restrictions have been imposed. In 1988, especially, new laws resulted in a 19 percent drop in the number of legal gun owners.

During that same period, overall violent crime increased by 29 percent.

The most dramatic example is Australia. In the twenty-five years leading up to 1996, incidents of armed robbery and homicides with guns steadily decreased. In that year, extremely strict gun laws were instituted. Citizens of Australia turned in 640,381 personal firearms. One year later, homicides were up 3.2 percent. Assaults were up 8.6 percent. Armed robberies increased 44 percent. Break-ins and the assaults on the elderly increased.

Even in the United States, we have an experiment in gun control. Washington D.C., our nation's capital, has had a ban on guns for more than twenty-five years. The result has been a steady increase in violent crime. The city has the highest murder rate in the nation. Colbert I. King, columnist for *The Washington Post*, tried to explain the constant increase in a 2003 editorial. "Experts are still trying to sort out the reasons." He thought the reason was pretty clear, however. "Clearly the prevalence of handguns – and people willing to use them – has a great deal to do with it." But supposedly, the ban on guns was going to remove those weapons. Apparently experience has proven that when guns are outlawed, only outlaws will have guns.

All of this indicates that there is a valid self-defense concern attached to gun control. The more guns are brought under government control, the less self-defense there is possible. In the words of Alexander Hamilton:

> *Little more can reasonably be aimed at, with respect to the people at large, than to have them properly armed and equipped.*

[1] Davis, *George Washington and the American Revolution*, pg. 269.

[2] Scheer and Rankin, *Rebels and Redcoats*, pg. 352.

[3] *Baron von Steuben's Revolutionary War Drill Manual*, pg. 1-2.

[4] Scheer and Rankin, *Rebels and Redcoats*, pg. 355.

[5] Hogg and Batchelor, *Armies of the American Revolution*, pg. 57.

[6] Fleming, *Now We Are Enemies*, pg. 230.

[7] Muir, *Tactics and the Experience of Battle in the Age of Napoleon*, pg. 78.

[8] Oman, *Wellington's Army, 1809-1814*, pg. 77.

[9] Nafziger, *A Guide to Napoleonic Warfare*, pg. 2.

[10] Muir, *Tactics and the Experience of Battle in the Age of Napoleon*, pg. 81.

[11] Nosworthy, *With Musket, Cannon and Sword*, pg. 204-205.

[12] Fleming, *Now That We Are Enemies*, pg. 233.

[13] Hughes, *Firepower*, pg. 98-99.

[14] Fleming, *Now We Are Enemies*, pg. 232.

[15] *Ibid.*, pg. 233-234.

[16] Davis, *George Washington and the American Revolution*, pg. 291-292.

[17] Bowen, *Miracle at Philadelphia*, pg. 44.

[18] *Ibid.*, pg. 45.

[19] Malcomlm, *To Keep and Bear Arms*, pg. 9.

[20] *Ibid.*, pg. 10.

[21] *Ibid.*, pg. 16.

[22] *Ibid.*, pg. 18.

[23] *Ibid.*, pg. 22.

[24] *Ibid.*, pg. 42-43.

[25] *Ibid.*, pg. 77-78.

[26] *Ibid.*, pg. 80.

[27] *Ibid.*, pg. 110.

[28] *Ibid.*, pg. 113.

[29] *Ibid.*, pg. 114.

[30] *Ibid.*, pg. 115.

[31] *Ibid.*, pg. 116.

[32] *Ibid.*, pg. 117.

[33] *Ibid.*, pg. 122.

[34] *Ibid.*, pg. 134.

[35] *Ibid.*, pg. 156.

★★★★★

Individual Right #13

The Right To Consent To Government

★★★★★

Responsibility #13

Vote

★★★★★

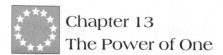

Chapter 13
The Power of One

Let each citizen remember at the moment he is offering his vote that he is not making a present or a compliment to please an individual – or at least that he ought not so to do; but that he is executing one of the most solemn trusts in human society for which he is accountable to God and his country. (Samuel Adams)

The 2000 presidential election drove home the importance of individual voting. George W. Bush lost the popular vote but won the Electoral College by 271 votes to 266 for challenger Al Gore. To win the election required 270. The ballots in Florida were too close to call and resulted in seemingly endless recounts that kept the results in limbo for over a month after the election. New Mexico and Oregon were just as tight but they resolved the count within a few days. Ultimately, Bush won New Mexico by a mere 366 votes and Florida by only 537. More significant than the narrow margin in the vote was the fact that over two and a half million registered voters in Florida didn't vote. (8,752,717 registered to 5,962,657 votes actually cast) A very small percentage of them could have changed the outcome.

But Arizona may have the record for close races. In 1992, there were two seats open for the new District 6. Three candidates ran for those seats, Laurie Daniels, Richard Kyle and John Gaylord. The two of those three who received the most votes would win the seats.

When all the votes were counted, Daniels easily won the first seat. However, Kyle and Gaylord ended up with precisely the same number of votes. A recount was mandated. The recount gave a different total number of votes, but it was still a tie. Another recount gave yet a third total, but the candidates were still tied.

According to Arizona law, once three counts were made, the matter was decided by a game of chance. Kyle and Gaylord agreed to cut a deck of cards. Kyle drew first and got a three of diamonds. He was sure that he had lost, but Gaylord then pulled a two, giving the election to Kyle.

The ironic part of the whole affair was that Gaylord's wife had failed to vote. She had been too busy that day and, figuring that one vote didn't matter, she just never found time to do it. She wasn't alone, however. There were 30,000 other voters who failed to make it to the polls that day. Any one of them would have decided the election.[1]

An individual vote matters far more than most people think. When you average out the totals for the election of John F. Kennedy, he won by one vote per precinct across the country. Most local ballot issues are decided by a very small percentage of the voters in that area. In Arizona, where this ministry is located, three of the seats in the State Legislature were decided in the last election by less than one hundred votes. Your vote actually does matter.

Small States vs. Large States

The Founding Fathers spent a great deal of time trying to make the election process as equitable as possible. The whole issue of representation was uppermost in their thinking.

We have already seen how different the states were from each other. It is nothing short of a miracle that the nation survived those first years. They squabbled constantly with each other, threatened each other, argued and occasionally even threatened to secede from the Confederation of States. It proved nearly impossible to get anything done. The government was unable to raise any money. Our ambassadors to other nations were either laughed at or ignored. The delegates to the Constitutional Convention knew that if they did not do something drastic, the United States would probably not be united for very long.

If they did not do something drastic, the United States would probably not be united very long.

The very first day, Edmund Randolph, the governor of Virginia, stood up and proposed a whole new national government, consisting of a national executive, a national judiciary and a national legislature made up of two houses, one elected by the people, the other elected by the first house. It became known as the Virginia Plan.[2]

The biggest question was how the states would be represented in each of the legislative branches. The debate lasted through half the summer and nearly split the Convention more than once.

A delegate from New Jersey, Judge Brearly, stood up on Saturday, June 9, and defended the position of his state. He pointed out that a large state like Virginia would swallow up small states like New Jersey and Georgia if the number of delegates in the new government was determined by the population of the state. Virginia would have sixteen votes while Georgia had one. The small states would always be outvoted and their interest would not be protected. He felt that each state should have a single vote in the new government.[3]

James Wilson from Pennsylvania responded, "Shall New Jersey have the same right or council in the nation with Pennsylvania? I say no! It is unjust."[4] He and the delegates from other large states did not want a small state to be able to dictate anything to them.

Roger Sherman proposed the compromise that eventually enabled everyone to agree. He suggested that votes be conducted both ways. In the first branch, the House, each state would be represented by a number of delegates determined by the population of the state. In the second branch, the Senate, each state would have one vote.[5]

The idea was not embraced immediately. In fact, it was debated for another month. But on July 16, it was decided to give each state two votes in the Senate and representation in the House proportional to the population.[6] The small states were given equal voice so that their needs would be acknowledged and the large states were given proportional representation so that they would not be restricted by the small states.

The Electoral College

This was the idea behind the Electoral College. Each state has different needs determined by geographical location and cultural background, and the Founding Fathers wanted representation in an election to be balanced in the same way that the two branches of Congress were. They recognized that in a general election, the larger states would overwhelm the smaller states to such an extent that the small states would not even be noticed.

Instead of just counting the total number of votes for president, each state would vote for electors who would then cast their votes for the president. The number of electors that each state was allowed was one for each representative in the House and one for each Senator. That meant that every state had at least three Electoral College votes.

It was left up to the states to determine how those electors were selected. Generally all the electors vote for the candidate who wins the popular vote in the state. There are some exceptions. In Maine and Nebraska, for example, the candidate who wins in each congressional district gets that vote and the candidate who wins the entire state gets the remaining two votes.

The largest state population is in California with a little over 33 million. The smallest is Wyoming with 479,602. The two states are very different. Wyoming does not have any of the kind of population centers that can be found in southern California. Candidates who focused on just the 33 million people in California would be likely to ignore the half a million in Wyoming.

California has fifty-five electoral votes and Wyoming has three. That means that each electoral vote in Wyoming represents about 160,000 residents while each vote in California represents a little over 600,000. The Electoral College gives Wyoming a little more say to balance out the low population.

There are two sets of interests involved – those of the individual people and those of the state or region. The Founding Fathers devised an ingenious system to balance the needs of both.[7]

The system was designed to give the best representation in government to every citizen. Without it, candidates would focus all of their attention on the largest population centers and ignore more rural areas. There would be no reason for them to address any of the issues outside of the major cities. Campaigns would turn into television advertising and we would never find out most of what a candidate believes.

The Electoral College has worked well for over two hundred years. Most people today have gotten the mistaken idea that the Electoral College was created simply because the Founders didn't trust the average voter. The reality is that they were concerned with protecting regional interests. It was the difference between pure democracy and a republic, and it works just as effectively as the division of the Congress into two branches. No population center can easily impose its interests at the expense of any other area.

Pure democracy cannot subsist long nor be carried far into the departments of state – it is very subject to caprice and the madness of popular rage. (John Witherspoon)

Black Voting Rights

The Constitutional Convention spent most of the time arguing over representation so that no single group of people or region of the country would be able to dominate another. They wanted balance.

As we noted earlier, however, that doesn't mean that everything started out perfect. There were large groups that were still not represented. Most notable were the black slaves in the south and women everywhere. It took many years and a civil war before they were allowed to participate.

There were some state constitutions that protected voting rights for free black men as early as 1776. Delaware, Maryland, New Hampshire, New York, Pennsylvania and Massachusetts all had such laws by 1784. As slavery became the driving political issue, some states began to limit voting to whites only. Maryland made the change in 1809, for example.[8]

In May, 1854, the new Republican Party was formed, primarily as an anti-slavery party. This brought them into direct conflict with the pro-slavery Democrats, who were especially strong in the South. The elections of 1856 and 1860 were very much a choice between pro-slavery Democrats and anti-slavery Republicans. It was on this platform that Abraham Lincoln became president.

Of course, slavery was not the only issue involved in the war but it was a very significant one. And the elimination of slavery was a direct result of the war. At the end of the war, in 1865, a Republican Congress was able to pass the Thirteenth Amendment, which abolished slavery, and the Fourteenth Amendment, which gave full civil rights to blacks.

In the aftermath of the war, Rebels were not allowed to vote on the basis of Article III of the Constitution. Since most of them were Democrats, the Republicans easily gained control of the state legislatures in the South. And virtually every African-American was a Republican. As a result, many black legislators were elected. For example, there were forty-two in Texas, fifty in South Carolina, 127 in Louisiana and ninety-nine in Alabama.[9]

As the Rebels were given amnesty, they began to assert their influence in the political area again and the resistance to black voters grew in force and in violence. The Ku Klux Klan was formed by Democrats as a means of organizing efforts to oppose all black candidates.

The violence escalated as time went by. Democrats attacked the Republican Convention in Louisiana in 1866, killing sixty, both black and white, and wounding 150. Twenty-eight black legislators in Georgia were expelled on the claim that, even though they could vote, they could not hold office. As the Democrats regained control of the states, they repealed most of the civil rights laws that had been passed and installed in their place a series of laws designed to make it as difficult as possible for blacks to vote.[10]

These included poll taxes, a requirement that a voter pay a fee before he was allowed to vote. The fees were always made high enough that most blacks could not pay them. Literacy tests were applied, often with as much as twenty pages of information that blacks would not be likely to know, since as slaves they had never been given much education.[11]

There were "Grandfather" clauses, which allowed a person to vote only if his father or grandfather had been registered prior to the passage of the Fifteenth Amendment. Some ballots were made complex and misleading. In many places Black Codes, also known as "Jim Crow" laws, were instituted to restrict the freedoms and economic opportunities of blacks so that they would be prohibited from voting, holding office or owning property.[12] Many states began to have white only primaries.[13] The violence primarily included simple intimidation but lynchings became common. Between 1882 and 1964, there were 4,743 persons lynched across the South.[14]

Eisenhower started a civil rights commission to focus attention on the problem.

Not much changed until well into the twentieth century. President Dwight D. Eisenhower proposed civil rights legislation that would protect black voting rights. The versions that passed were watered down significantly. But Eisenhower started a civil rights commission to focus attention on the problem.

In 1963, President John F. Kennedy proposed a strong civil rights bill, using language taken from Eisenhower's original bill. Kennedy's assassination stopped the bill but momentum was increasing. In 1964, the Twenty-fourth Amendment was ratified, abolishing poll taxes. The party lines were still prominent in the vote. Ninety-one percent of the Republicans in Congress voted to end the poll tax but only seventy-one percent of the Democrats. In the Senate, fifteen of the sixteen opposed to ending the poll tax were Democrats.[15]

Democratic President Lyndon B. Johnson took up Kennedy's civil rights bill. He had to work closely with Republicans in the House to get it passed. Only 198 out of the 315 Democrats supported him. In the Senate, 97 percent of the Republicans voted for the bill. Seventeen of the eighteen senators opposed to the bill were Democrats.[16]

The 1965 Voting Rights Act ended most of the impediments to black voters. It banned literacy tests and allowed the federal government to oversee voter registration. By the end of the century, it could not be said that racism had been eliminated but at least voting rights were relatively secure.

Remember the Ladies

John and Abigail Adams corresponded regularly when they were apart. Abigail had occasion frequently to give political advise to her husband. While he was in Philadelphia in 1776, working toward the Declaration of Independence, she sent him a request and a warning.

> *I long to hear that you have declared an independency – and by the way in the new Code of Laws which I suppose it will be necessary for you to make I desire you would Remember the Ladies, and be more generous and favourable to them than your ancestors. Do not put such unlimited power into the hands of the Husbands. Remember all men would be tyrants if they could. If perticuliar care and attention is not paid to the Ladies we are determined to foment a Rebelion, and will not hold ourselves bound by any Laws in which we have no voice, or Representation.*

John Adams replied in the good-natured humor that he and Abigail shared so passionately.

As to your extraordinary Code of Laws, I cannot but laugh. We have been told that our Struggle has loosened the bands of Government every where. That Children and Apprentices were disobedient – that schools and Colledges were grown turbulent – that Indians slighted their Guardians and Negroes grew insolent to their Masters. But your Letter was the first Intimation that another Tribe more numerous and powerfull than all the rest were grown discontented. – This is rather too coarse a Compliment but you are so saucy, I wont blot it out.

Good-natured or not, he caught a glimpse of the future. As America grew, women began to wonder why they were not extended all of the rights that were in the Constitution. Early in the nineteenth century they began to speak up. The movement grew in strength until they could no longer be ignored.

Susan B. Anthony was one of the first names to become associated with women's suffrage. In 1837, she asked for equal pay for women teachers, a precursor of the twentieth century drive for an Equal Rights Amendment.

It was in 1848 that the movement began to gain some organization. A convention was held in Seneca Falls, New York, in July of that year. That week started a movement that seventy years later resulted in passage of the Nineteenth Amendment, giving women the right to vote. The women's suffrage movement did not attract the violence that civil rights did, but it still was resisted.

On November 5, 1872, Susan B. Anthony, along with some other women, tried to vote and was arrested. The publicity began to gain support for the movement. In 1893, Colorado passed a referendum that gave women the vote. Other states gradually began to follow suit.

One incident of interest occurred in 1855. Lucy Stone and Henry Blackwell were married in a nontraditional ceremony. They renounced the legal authority of a husband over a wife and Stone kept her last name.

That legal authority was common to most cultures in the world. And America was no different at the time. A woman was not allowed to vote. She was considered by the courts to be "civilly dead." She could not testify in court, something that even slaves were allowed to do. Women were considered by most men to be incapable of understanding politics well enough to vote. The idea of having a woman involved in politics was unthinkable. Albert Gallatin, the Secretary of the Treasury under Thomas Jefferson, once suggested that some women be appointed to government posts. Jefferson replied, "The appointment of a woman to office is an innovation for which the public is not prepared, nor am I." Needless to say, Lucy Stone's wedding created quite a bit of talk around the nation.

Women were considered by most men to be incapable of understanding politics well enough to vote.

It did not help any that the subservience of women had a religious foundation. The Seneca Falls Convention was inspired by the experience of some women who opposed slavery. Sarah and Angelina Grimke, in 1836, began traveling around New England to speak against slavery. They aroused the anger of the Council of Congregational Ministers of Massachusetts, who issued a statement condemning them.

> *The power of a woman is her dependency flowing from the consciousness of that weakness which God has given her for her protection . . . when she assumes the place and tone of man as a public reformer, she yields the power which God has given her for her protection and her character becomes unnatural.*[17]

Several women made plans to attend an anti-slavery convention in London. Some clergy got there ahead of them and warned the organizers that the women actually intended to speak. The decision was made to allow them to attend, as long as they remained quiet and sat behind a curtained area. This incident shocked enough women to bring them to action, and the Seneca Falls Convention was planned to explore women's rights.[18]

All of this was based on an erroneous reading of a few biblical passages. Women were the "weaker partner," and therefore considered frivolous. Women were to be silent in the church and therefore should be silent everywhere. Women were to be submitted to their husbands and therefore should not be allowed to participate in any area of public activity.

The problem is that the Bible never says those things. The woman is physically weaker, but that only means that men have the capability of forcing them into submission. It does not mean that men should force them into anything, only that they are able to do so. A few chapters before Paul says that women should be silent in church (1 Corinthians 14:34), he refers to women who were praying and prophesying in church

302   Me, My Country, My God

without any hint that he thought they should stop (1 Corinthians 11:5). He said that women should be silent and be submissive because of what the law says (1 Corinthians 14:34). The problem is that the Old Testament Law never says that. Paul was referring to Roman law, which did not allow women to speak in public. That law is not valid in America.

This is not the place for an extensive study of this subject but we must note that the Bible gives the wife authority over her husband just as much as it gives the husband authority over the wife.

> *The wife does not have authority over her own body, but the husband does. And likewise the husband does not have authority over his own body, but the wife does.* (1 Corinthians 7:4)

The biblical evidence shows that Jesus treated women as equals rather than talking down to them. He defied the standards of his day to validate the lives of women. Even Paul, who is generally accused of being a woman-hater spoke with approval of women in leadership positions in the church. Phoebe and Priscilla are examples and one woman, Junia, was even called an apostle (Romans 16:7).

There was never a justification for withholding the unalienable rights of a woman any more valid than the excuses given for withholding them from the black slaves. True Christianity brings life to the individual. The Constitution of the United States is in agreement with that.

It is a sad thing that it took so long for women to gain such a simple right as voting. But at least they do have it now. Abigail Adams proved to be right.

I can not say I think you very generous to the Ladies, for whilst you are proclaiming peace and good will to Men, Emancipating all Nations, you insist upon retaining an absolute power over Wives. But you must remember that Arbitrary power is like most other things which are very hard, very liable to be broken – and notwithstanding all your wise Laws and Maxims we have it in our power not only to free ourselves but to subdue our Masters, and without violence throw both your natural and legal authority at our feet.

---

[1] This story was related by Jeff Groscost, former Arizona Speaker of the House.

[2] Bowen, *Miracle at Philadelphia*, pg. 38.

[3] *Ibid.*, pg. 84.

[4] *Ibid.*, pg. 85.

[5] *Ibid.*, pg. 94.

[6] *Ibid.*, pg. 117.

[7] For a good explanation of the Electoral College, see www.wallbuilders.com.

[8] Barton, *A History of Black Voting Rights*, pg. 4-5.

[9] *Ibid.*, pg. 8.

[10] *Ibid.*, pg. 8-9.

[11] *Ibid.*, pg. 11.

[12] *Ibid.*, pg. 12.

[13] *Ibid.*, pg. 14.

[14] *Ibid.*, pg. 15.

[15] *Ibid.*, pg. 23.

[16] *Ibid.*, pg. 24.

[17] Stone, *When God Was a Woman*, pg. 232.

[18] *Ibid.*

 Conclusion

The United States has been called a Christian nation from its inception. This does not mean that the Founders of America were perfect. Listening to evangelicals, it is easy to get the idea that they all carried Bibles around with them and preached to anyone who would let them. Listening to others, it is easy to get the idea that the Founders all were atheists and spent most of their time involved in sexual infidelities.

The truth lies somewhere between those extremes. Unfortunately, when most people think of the Founders, there are only a few names that come to mind – Washington, Adams, Franklin, Jefferson. There were many more than that who participated in the passing of the Declaration of Independence and in the Constitutional Convention. And many of them were very devout. Charles Pinckney and John Langdon founded the American Bible Society. James McHenry founded the Baltimore Bible Society. Abraham Baldwin, Roger Sherman, William Samuel Johnson, John Dickinson and Jacob Broom were all known at the time as theological writers. Noah Webster, famous for producing his *Dictionary of the English Language*, also created a modern translation of the entire Bible. A large number of the signers of the Declaration were full-fledged evangelicals.

But the focus of modern Americans is usually on the four or five well-known Founders, and claims are made that they were all deists. For the most part they were. Does this mean that America is not Christian?

If we apply the criteria that modern evangelicals use for "Christian," the acceptance of Jesus as Savior with the sinner's prayer, some of these men do not appear very "born again." Eighty-three year old Benjamin Franklin was asked by a good friend, Ezra Stiles, for a statement of his Christian convictions. He was politely ambiguous.

> *Here is my Creed. I believe in one God, Creator of the Universe: That he governs the World by his Providence. That he ought to be worshipped. That the most acceptable Service we can render to him, is doing good to his other Children. That the Soul of Man is immortal, and will be treated with Justice in another Life, respect[ing] its Conduct in this. These I take to be the fundamental Principles of all sound Religion, and I regard them as you do, in whatever Sect I meet with them.* [1]

Stiles wasn't satisfied with the answer, so he pressed Franklin for some details. Was he a Christian or not? Franklin said that he believed Jesus had given the world the best system of morals and religion that had ever been seen but he believed those morals had "received various corrupting changes." Regarding the divinity of Jesus, however, he was not sure.

> *I have, with most of the present Dissenters in Engl[an]d, some Doubts . . . tho' it is a Question I do not dogmatize upon, hav[ing] never studied*

it, & think it needless to busy myself with it now,
when I expect soon an Opport[unity] of know[ing]
the Truth with less Trouble.[2]

Franklin died a few weeks later. Presumably he found out.

Thomas Jefferson did not believe in the divinity of Jesus any more than Franklin. Through the last years of his life, he spent some time creating what came to be known as *The Jefferson Bible*. He purchased copies of the New Testament and cut out the parts that he considered to be valid, thus eliminating the parts he thought to be corruptions of later writers. He removed every reference to the miraculous, feeling that such stories were mere superstition.

When it was printed, he included a statement on the cover page that it was "an abridgment of the New Testament for the use of the Indians, unembarrassed with matters of fact or faith beyond the level of their comprehensions." But he was under considerable attack by his critics for being an "atheist" and, though he never intended the printed copy of the book to be given to the public, he seemed to be making a statement that would protect him just in case. His real motives, and a good idea of his beliefs, can be seen in the letters he wrote to several friends while he was working on the project, particularly Dr. Benjamin Rush, Dr. Joseph Priestly and John Adams. This sample from a letter to Adams on October 13, 1813, gives a good summary.

We must reduce our volume to the simple
evangelists, select, even from them, the very words
only of Jesus, paring off the amphiboligisms into

which they have been led, by forgetting often, or not understanding what had fallen from him, by giving their own misconceptions as his dicta, and expressing unintelligibly for others what they had not understood themselves. There will be found remaining the most sublime and benevolent code of morals which has ever been offered to man. I have performed this operation for my own use, by cutting verse by verse out of the printed book, and by arranging the matter which is evidently his, and which is as distinguishable as diamonds in a dunghill. The result is an octavo of forty-six pages, of pure and unsophisticated doctrines, such as were professed and acted on by the unlettered Apostles, the Apostolic Fathers, and the Christians of the first century.[3]

What remained was a Jesus who was stripped of anything divine or miraculous. In Jefferson's mind, he was a good man with a sublime set of morals that he tried to teach.

John Adams was a Presbyterian, but his letters indicate he was not so sure that Christianity was the only way to God. In one letter, for example, he said that he could not believe "that all these millions and millions of men are to be miserable and only a handful of Elect Calvinists happy forever."[4] Generally he seemed to agree with Jefferson, though he was less critical of the traditional church doctrines.

Washington's religious beliefs are difficult to determine. He rarely indicated much of his thinking. He wrote in 1795, "In politics as in religion, my tenets are few and simple."[5] He spoke often of God but rarely called Him God.

He used terms such as "Providence," "the Grand Architect of the Universe," "the Governor of the Universe," "Higher Cause," "Great Ruler of Events," "All Wise Creator," and "the Supreme Dispenser of all Good." He definitely believed in God but seemed to view Him as a distant and aloof personality who could not be easily approached.

We say all of this to point out that in many ways, early America was not much different than today. There were tremendous arguments over theology that raged through the society. There were many who did not have a belief in the divinity of Jesus. There were many who were as evangelical as anyone today. When we say that America was founded as a Christian nation, we are not denying the fact that many were not Christian in the narrow sense that we often think of it.

We are saying, however, that they all had a firm belief in a creator and that the individual rights that we possess and for which they dedicated their lives and everything they owned, came from that creator and not from any government. They also believed in an absolute right and wrong that were not dependant on the vote of the majority. Right and wrong transcended law. Even the most "unchristian" of the Founding Fathers were guided by a belief in God that was the foundation of everything they did. John Adams spoke for them all in his old age.

> *I say that if I had not steadfastly believed in a Government of the Universe, wise beyond my conception, I should have been constantly not only in dejection but in despair, for at least 55 years of my life.*

If America ever finds any reason for despair, it will be because we have lost sight of that "Government of the Universe," wise beyond our conception. "We the people" who consent to this "government of the people, by the people and for the people" are what will keep despair from ever being a part of our experience as a nation. The principles of this great nation, illustrated so often by our Founders and by the history of this nation, are as valid as ever. But living in the freedom and the individual rights that we have also means that we live with the responsibilities for those freedoms. To continue enjoying freedom, we must not forget that we must have character. We must have virtue. We must persist in prayer for this nation and for those who lead us. We must educate ourselves and learn to reason. We must protect the sanctity of the family. We must recognize the equality of all people and do all that we can to preserve their right to life and liberty. We must develop and keep a work ethic that produces the wealth on which America rests. We must always know the truth, not just the headlines, and we must always be willing to stand for truth, even when it is not popular. We must recognize that we cannot isolate ourselves forever from the rest of the world. The blessings that we possess give us a responsibility to share life with the world. We must participate; at the very least, we must vote.

It is no small thing to be a citizen of the greatest nation on earth. And this is still the greatest nation on earth. Let us all resolve to do our part to keep it that way.

---

[1]Gaustad, *Neither King nor Prelate*, pg. 65.

[2]*Ibid.*, pg. 66.

[3]*The Jefferson Bible*, pg. 17.

[4]Gaustad, *Neither King nor Prelate*, pg. 96.

[5]*Ibid.*, pg. 76.

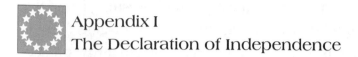

Appendix I
The Declaration of Independence

IN CONGRESS, July 4, 1776

The unanimous Declaration of the thirteen united States of America.

When in the Course of human events, it becomes necessary for one people to dissolve the political bands which have connected them with another, and to assume among the powers of the earth, the separate and equal station to which the Laws of Nature and of Nature's God entitle them, a decent respect to the opinions of mankind requires that they should declare the causes which impel them to the Separation.

We hold these truths to be self-evident, that all men are created equal, that they are endowed by their Creator with certain unalienable Rights, that among these are Life, Liberty, and the Pursuit of Happiness–That to secure these rights, Governments are instituted among Men, deriving their just Powers from the consent of the governed, – That whenever any Form of Government becomes destructive of these ends, it is the Right of the People to alter or to abolish it, and to institute new Government, laying its foundation on such principles and organizing its powers in such form, as to them shall seem most likely to effect their Safety and Happiness. Prudence, indeed, will dictate that Governments long established should not be changed for light and transient causes; and accordingly all experience hath shewn, that mankind are more diposed to suffer, while evils are sufferable, than to right themselves by abolishing the forms to which they are accustomed. But when a long train of abuses and unsurpations, pursuing invariably the same Object evinces a design to reduce them under absolute Despotism, it is their Right, it is their duty, to throw off such Government, and to provide new Guards for their future security. – Such has been the patient sufferance of these Colonies; and such is now the necessity which constrains them to alter their former Systems of Government. The history of the present King of Great Britain is a history of repeated injuries and usurpations, all having in direct object the establishment of an absolute Tyranny over these States. To prove this, let Facts be submitted to a candid World.

He has refused his Assent to Laws, the most wholesome and necessary for the public good.

He has forbidden his Governors to pass Laws of immediate and pressing importance, unless suspended in their operation till his Assent should be obtained; and when so suspended, he has utterly neglected to attend to them.

He has refused to pass other Laws for the accommodation of large districts of people, unless those people would relinquish the right of Representation in the Legislature, a right inestimable to them and formidable to tyrants only.

He has called together legislative bodies at places unusual, uncomfortable, and distant from the depository of their public Records, for the sole purpose of fatiguing them into compliance with his measures.

He has dissolved Representative Houses repeatedly, for opposing with manly firmness his invasions on the rights of the People.

He has refused for a long time, after such dissolutions, to cause others to be elected; whereby the Legislative powers, incapable of Annihilation, have returned to the People at large for their exercise; the State remaining in the mean time exposed to all the dangers of invasion from without, and convulsions within.

He has endeavoured to prevent the population of these States; for that purpose obstructing the Laws for Naturalization of Foreigners; refusing to pass others to encourage their migrations hither, and raising the conditions of new Appropriations of Lands.

He has obstructed the Administration of Justice, by refusing his Assent to Laws for establishing Judiciary powers.

He has made Judges dependent on his Will alone, for the tenure of their offices, and the amount and payment of their salaries.

He has erected a multitude of New Offices, and sent hither swarms of Officers to harrass our people, and eat out their substance.

He has kept among us, in times of peace, Standing Armies without the Consent of our legislatures.

He has affected to render the Military independent of and superior to the Civil power.

He has combined with others to subject us to a jurisdiciton foreign to our constitution, and unacknowledged by our laws; giving his Assent to their Acts of pretended Legislation;

For Quartering large bodies of armed troops among us;

For protecting them, by a mock Trial, from punishment for any Murders which they should commit on the Inhabitants of these States;

For cutting off our Trade with all parts of the world;

For imposing Taxes on us without our Consent;

For depriving us in many cases, of the benefits of Trial by Jury;

For transporting us beyond Seas to be tried for pretended offences;

For abolishing the free System of English Laws in a neighbouring Province, establishing therein an Arbitrary government, and enlarging its Boundaries so as to render it at once an example and fit instrument for introducing the same absolute rule into these Colonies;

For taking away our Charters, abolishing our most valuable Laws, and altering fundamentally the Forms of our Governments;

For suspending our own Legislatures, and declaring themselves invested with power to legislate for us in all cases whatsoever.

He has abdicated Government here, by declaring us out of his Protection and waging War against us.

He has plundered our seas, ravaged our Coasts, burnt our towns, and destroyed the lives of our people.

He is at this time transporting large Armies of foreign Mercenaries to compleat the works of death, desolation and tyranny, already begun with circumstances of Cruelty & perfidy, scarcely paralleled in the most barbarous ages, and totally unworthy the Head of a civilized nation.

He has constrained our fellow Citizens taken Captive on the high Seas to bear Arms against their Country, to become the executioners of their friends and Brethren, or to fall themselves by their Hands.

He has excited domestic insurrections amongst us, and has endeavoured to bring on the inhabitants of our frontiers, the merciless Indian Savages, whose known rule of warfare, is an undistinguished destruction of all ages, sexes and conditions.

In every stage of these Oppressions We have Petitioned for Redress in the most humble terms; Our repeated Petitions have been answered only by repeated injury. A Prince whose character is thus marked by every act which may define a Tyrant, is unfit to be the ruler of a free people.

Nor have We been wanting in attentions to our British brethren. We have warned them from time to time of attempts by their legislature to extend an unwarrantable jurisdiction over us. We have reminded them of the circumstances of our emigration and settlement here. We have appealed to their native justice and magnanimity, and we have conjured them by the ties of our common kindred to disavow these usurpations, which, would inevitably interrupt our connections and correspondence. They too have been deaf to the voice of justice and of consanguinity. We must, therefore, acquiesce in the necessity, which denounces our Separation, and hold them, as we hold the rest of mankind, Enemies in War, in Peace, Friends.

We, therefore, the Representatives of the united States of America, in General Congress, Assembled, appealing to the

Supreme Judge of the world for the rectitude of our intentions, do, in the Name, and by Authority of the good People of these Colonies, solemnly publish and declare, That these United Colonies are, and of Right ought to be Free and Independent States; that they are Absolved from all Allegiance to the British Crown, and that all political connection between them and the State of Great Britain, is and ought to be totally dissolved; and that as Free and Independent States, they have full Power to levy War, conclude Peace, contract Alliances, establish Commerce, and to do all other Acts and Things which Independent States may of right do. And for the support of this Declaration, with a firm reliance on the protection of divine Providence, we mutually pledge to each other our Lives, our Fortunes and our sacred Honor.

(The signatures of the signers appear in the original in six columns.)

Column 1
>   Georgia: Button Gwinnett
>   Lyman Hall
>   George Walton

Column 2
>   North Carolina: William Hooper
>   Joseph Hewes
>   John Penn
>   South Carolina: Edward Rutledge
>   Thomas Heyward, Jr.
>   Thomas Lynch, Jr.
>   Arthur Middleton

Column 3

Massachusetts	John Hancock
Maryland:	Samuel Chase
	William Paca
	Thomas Stone
	Charles Carroll of
	Carrollton
Virginia:	George Wythe
	Richard Henry Lee
	Thomas Jefferson
	Benjamin Harrison
	Thomas Nelson, Jr.
	Francis Lightfoot Lee
	Carter Braxton

Column 4

Pennsylvania:	Robert Morris
	Benjamin Rush
	Benjamin Franklin
	John Morton
	George Clymer
	James Smith
	George Taylor
	James Wilson
	George Ross
Delaware:	Caesar Rodney
	George Read
	Thomas McKean

Column 5

New York:	William Floyd
	Philip Livingston
	Francis Lewis
	Lewis Morris
New Jersey:	Richard Stockton
	John Witherspoon
	Francis Hopkinson
	John Hart
	Abraham Clark

Column 6

New Hampshire:	Josiah Bartlett
	William Whipple
Massachusetts:	Samuel Adams
	John Adams
	Robert Treat Paine
	Elbridge Gerry
Rhode Island:	Stephen Hopkins
	William Ellery
Connecticut:	Roger Sherman
	Samuel Huntington
	William Williams
	Oliver Wolcott
New Hampshire:	Matthew Thornton

 Bibliography

Allison, Robert J. *The Crescent Obscured, The United States and the Muslim World, 1776-1815*. Oxford University Press. New York. 1995. 266 pgs.

Andrews, James and David Zarefsky. *American Voices, Significant Speeches in American History, 1640-1945*. Longman. New York. 1989. 506 pgs.

Andrist, Ralph K. (Editor). *The Founding Fathers, George Washington, a Biography in His Own Words, Volume 1*. Newsweek. New York. 1972. 208 pgs.

Baepler, Paul (Editor). *White Slaves, African Masters, An Anthology of American Barbary Captivity Narratives*. The University of Chicago Press. Chicago. 1999. 310 pgs.

Barton, David. *A History of Black Voting Rights*. The WallBuilder Report. (www.wallbuilders.com)

Bennett, William J. (Editor). *Our Country's Founders, A Book of Advice for Young People*. Broadman & Holman Publishers. 1998. 314 pgs.

Bennett, William J. (Editor). *Our Sacred Honor, Words of Advice from the Founders in Stories, Letters, Poems, and Speeches*. Simon and Schuster. New York. 1997. 430 pgs.

Boller, Paul F., Jr. *Presidential Campaigns, From George Washington to George W. Bush.* Oxford University Press. New York. 2004. 479 pgs.

Boorstin, Daniel. *The Lost World of Thomas Jefferson.* Beacon Press. Boston. 1948. 306 pgs.

Bowen, Catherine Drinker. *Miracle at Philadelphia, The Story of the Constitutional Convention, May to September 1787.* Atlantic Monthly Press, Little, Brown and Company. Boston. 1966. 346 pgs.

Bowen, Catherine Drinker. *The Most Dangerous Man in America, Scenes from the Life of Benjamin Franklin.* An Atlantic Monthly Press Book, Little, Brown and Company. Boston. 1974. 274 pgs.

Brookhiser, Richard (Editor). *Rules of Civility.* The Free Press. New York. 1997. 90 pgs.

Burke, Theresa, Ph.D. with David C. Reardon, Ph.D. *Forbidden Grief, The Unspoken Pain of Abortion.* Acorn Books. Springfield, Illinois. 2002. 327 pgs.

Church, F. Forrester (Editor). *The Jefferson Bible, The Life and Morals of Jesus of Nazareth.* Beacon Press. Boston. 1989. 171 pgs.

Cobb, Richard (General Editor) and Colin Jones (Editor). *Voices of the French Revolution.* Salem House Publishers. Topsfield, Massachusetts. 1988. 256 pgs.

Cook, Blanche Wiesen, and Alice Kessler Harris and Ronald Radosh. *Past Imperfect, Alternative Essays in American History, Volume 1: from Colonial Times to the Civil War.* Alfred A Knopf. New York. 1973. 289 pgs.

Davis, Burke. *George Washington and the American Revolution.* Random House. New York. 1975. 497 pgs.

Douglas, William O. *The Bible and the Schools.* Little, Brown and Company. Boston. 1966. 65 pgs.

D'Souza, Dinesh. *What's So Great About America.* Penguin Books. New York. 2002. 218 pgs.

Durant, Will and Ariel. *The Age of Napoleon, A History of European Civilization from 1789 to 1815.* Simon and Schuster. New York. 1975. 872 pgs.

Edersheim, Alfred. *The Temple, Its Ministry and Services.* Hendrickson Publishers. Peabody, Massachusetts. 1994. 340 pgs.

Ferris, Robert G. and James H. Charleton. *The Signers of the Constitution.* Interpretive Publications, Inc. Flagstaff, Arizona. 1986. 268 pgs.

Fischer, David Hackett. *Albion's Seed, Four British Folkways in America.* Oxford University Press. New York. 1989. 946 pgs.

Fleming, Thomas J. *Now We Are Enemies, The Story of Bunker Hill.* St. Martin's Press. New York. 1960. 366 pgs.

Franklin, Benjamin. *The Autobiography of Benjamin Franklin.* Wordsworth American Library. Ware, Herfordshire. 1996. 208 pgs.

Gatto, John Taylor. *The Underground History of American Education, A Schoolteacher's Intimate Investigation Into The Problem Of Modern Schooling.* The Oxford Village Press. New York. 2001. 412 pgs.

Gaustad, Edwin S. *Neither King nor Prelate, Religion and the New Nation, 1776-1826.* William B. Eerdmans Publishing Company. Grand Rapids, Michigan. 1993. 196 pgs.

Gaylin, Willard, M.D. *The Male Ego.* Viking Penguin. New York. 1992. 276 pgs.

Greenberg, Ellen. *The Supreme Court Explained.* W. W. Norton & Company. New York. 1997. 208 pgs.

Gross, Robert A. *The Minutemen and Their World.* Hill And Wang. New York. 1976. 242 pgs.

Hauply, Denis. *"A Convention of Delegates," The Creation of the Constitution.* Atheneum. New York. 1987. 148 pgs.

Hogg, Ian V. and John H. Batchelor. *Armies of the American Revolution.* Prentice-Hall Inc. Englewood Cliffs, New Jersey. 1975. 158 pgs.

Hughes, Major-General B.P., C.B., C.B.E. *Firepower, Weapons Effectiveness on the Battlefield, 1630-1850.* Arms and Armour Press. London. 1974. 174 pgs.

Jaffa, Harry V. with Bruce Ledewitz, Robert L. Stone, and George Anastaplo. *Original Intent and the Framers of the Constitution, A Disputed Question.* Regnery Publishing. Washington, D.C. 1994. 408 pgs.

Jeffrey, George. *Tactics and Grand Tactics of the Napoleonic Wars.* The Courier Publishing Co. Inc. 1982. 156 pgs.

Jones, Colin (Editor) and Richard Cobb (General Editor). *Voices of the French Revolution.* Salem House Publishers. Topsfield, Massachusetts. 1988. 256 pgs.

Katcher, Philip. *Armies of the American Wars 1753-1815.* Hastings House, Publishers. New York. 1975. 160 pgs.

Kepel, Gilles, Translated by Anthony F. Roberts. *Jihad: The Trail of Political Islam.* The Belknap Press of Harvard University Press. Cambridge, Massachusetts. 2002. 454 pgs.

Ketchum, Richard M. *Decisive Day, The Battle for Bunker Hill.* Doubleday & Company. Garden City, New York. 1962. 282 pgs.

Kramer, Lloyd S. (Editor). *Paine and Jefferson on Liberty.* A Frederick Ungar Book. Continuum. New York. 1988. 144 pgs.

Leahy, James E. *The First Amendment, 1791-1991, Two Hundred Years of Freedom.* McFarland & Company, Inc. Jefferson, North Carolina. 1991. 308 pgs.

Lee, John J., Jr. *The Producer's Business Handbook.* Focal Press. Boston. 2000. 173 pgs.

Locke, John. *A Letter Concerning Toleration.* William Benton, Publisher. Encyclopaedia Britannica, Inc. Chicago. 1952. 509 pgs.

Lockridge, Kenneth A. *A New England Town, The First Hundred Years.* W. W. Norton & Company, Inc. New York. 1970. 208 pgs.

Ludwig, Emil, translated by Eden and Cedar Paul. *Napoleon.* Garden City Publishing Company. Garden City, New York. 1926. 707 pgs.

Maier, Pauline. *The Old Revolutionaries, Political Lives in the Age of Samuel Adams.* W. W. Norton & Company. New York. 1980. 309 pgs.

Malcolm, Joyce Lee. *To Keep and Bear Arms, The Origins of an Anglo-American Right.* Harvard University Press. Cambridge, Massachusetts. 1994. 232 pgs.

Malone, Dumas. *The Story of the Declaration of Independence.* Oxford University Press. New York. 1954. 282 pgs.

Manning, John R. *The Story of Old Glory.* The Continuing Education Institute, Inc. Phoenix, Arizona. 1971. 48 pgs.

McDowell, Bart. *The Revolutionary War.* The National Geographic Society. Washington D.C. 1967. 199 pgs.

Miller, John C. *Origins of the American Revolution.* Stanford University Press. Stanford, California. 1943. 530 pgs.

Muir, Rory. *Tactics and the Experience of Battle in the Age of Napoleon.* Yale University Press. New Haven. 1998. 342 pgs.

Nafziger, G. F. *A Guide to Napoleonic Warfare, Maneuvers of the Battery, Battalion, and Brigade During the First Empire As Found in Contemporary Regulations.* Published by G. F. Nafziger. 294 pgs.

Nosworthy, Brent. *The Anatomy of Victory, Battle Tactics 1689-1783.* Hippocrene Books. New York. 1990. 395 pgs.

Nosworthy, Brent. *With Musket, Cannon and Sword, Battle Tactics of Napoleon and His Enemies.* Sarpedon. New York. 1996. 516 pgs.

Oman, Sir Charles. *Wellington's Army, 1809-1814.* Greenhill Books. London. 1913. 440 pgs.

Palmer, Dave R. *1794, America, Its Army, and the Birth of the Nation.* Presidio. Novato, California. 1994. 290 pgs.

Quint, Howard H. and Milton Cantor (Editors). *Men, Women, and Issues in American History, Volume I.* The Dorsey Press. Homewood, Illinois. 1975. 300 pgs.

Ralston, David B. *Importing the European Army, The Introduction of European Military Techniques and Institutions into the Extra-European World, 1600-1914.* The University of Chicago Press. Chicago. 1990. 198 pgs.

Randall, Willard Sterne. *Thomas Jefferson, A Life.* Henry Holt and Company. New York. 1993. 708 pgs.

Ramadon, Tariq. *Western Muslims and The Future of Islam.* Oxford University Press. Oxford. 2004. 272 pgs.

Reisser, Teri K., M.S., M.F.T. and Paul C. Reisser, M.D. *Healing After Abortion, Identifying and Overcoming Post-Abortion Syndrome.* Focus on the Family. 12 pgs.

Ridpath, John Clark. *James Otis The Pre-Revolutionist.* Kessinger Publishing. 111 pgs.

Ross, Steven. *From Flintlock to Rifle, Infantry Tactics, 1740-1866.* Associated University Press. London. 1979. 218 pgs.

Royster, Charles. *The Destructive War, William Tecumseh Sherman, Stonewall Jackson, and the Americans.* Alfred A. Knopf. New York. 1991. 523 pgs.

Schaeffer, Francis A. *How Should We Then Live? The Rise and Decline of Western Thought and Culture.* Fleming H. Revell Company. Old Tappan, New Jersey. 1976. 288 pgs.

Scheer, George F. and Hugh F. Rankin. *Rebels and Redcoats.* A Mentor Book published by the New American Library. New York. 1957. 639 pgs.

Schwartz, Bernard. *A History of the Supreme Court.* Oxford University Press. New York. 1993. 465 pgs.

Shakir, M. H. (Translator). *The Qur'an Translation.* Tahrike Tarsile Qur'an, Inc. Elmhurst, New York. 2003. 467 pgs.

Shenkman, Richard. *"I Love Paul Revere, Whether He Rode or Not".* HarperPerennial. New York. 1991. 226 pgs.

Shenkman, Richard. *Legends, Lies & Cherished Myths of American History.* William Morrow and Company, Inc. New York. 1988. 202 pgs.

Shenkman, Richard and Kurt Reiger. *One-Night Stands With American History, Odd, Amusing, and Little-Known Incidents.* Quill. New York. 1980. 285 pgs.

Sered, Susan Starr. *Priestess, Mother, Sacred Sister, Religions Dominated by Women.* Oxford University Press. New York. 1994. 330 pgs.

Seymour, Peter (Editor). *The Spirit of 1776, Life, Liberty and the Pursuit of Happiness During the American Revolution.* Hallmark Editions. Kansas City, Missouri. 1971. 61 pgs.

Stone, Merlin. *When God Was a Woman.* Dorset Press. New York. 1976. 265 pgs.

Syndar, Charles. *American Revolutionaries in the Making, Political Practices in Washington's Virginia.* The Free Press. New York. 1952. 160 pgs.

Tuchman, Barbara W. *The First Salute.* Alfred A. Knopf. New York. 1988. 347 pgs.

von Steuben, Baron Frederick William. *Baron von Steuben's Revolutionary War Drill Manual.* Dover Publications, Inc. New York. 1985. 161 pgs.

Wahlke, John C. (Editor). *The Causes of the American Revolution, Revised Edition.* D. C. Heath and Company. Boston. 1962. 131 pgs.

We the People . . ., a Secondary Level Student Text. National Bicentennial Competition on the Constitution and bill of Rights, Center for Civic Education. Calabasas, California. 1987. 164 pgs.

Wenham, Gordon J. *The New Interenational Commentary on the Old Testament, The Book of Leviticus.* William B. Eerdmans Publishing Company. Grand Rapids, Michigan. 1979. 362 pgs.

Whipple, A.B.C. *To the Shores of Tripoli, The Birth of the U.S. Navy and Marines.* William Morrow and Company, Inc. New York. 1991. 357 pgs.

Williams, Earl P. Jr. *What You Should Know About The American Flag.* Thomas Publications. Gettysburg, Pennsylvania. 1992. 52 pgs.

Williams, John Alden (Editor). *Great Religions of Modern Man, Islam.* George Braziller. New York. 1961. 256 pgs.

Index

Featured Products by Dr. C. Thomas and Pastor Maureen Anderson

BOOKS:

Becoming a Millionaire God's Way
Making Marriage a Love Story
90 Days to Health
Making Impossibilities Possible
Confessing God's Word
Discovering The Power of Confession
Wisdom Wins
Wisdom Wins 2

These and many other books, tapes and CD's are available from Living Word Bible Church. Order online at:

www.winners.tv

Or contact us at:
1-888-4WORDTV (1-888-496-7388)